MW01166850

PERRY'S
DEPARTMENT STORE

A Product Development Simulation

Karen M. Guthrie
VIRGINIA COMMONWEALTH UNIVERSITY

Rosalie Jackson Regni
VIRGINIA COMMONWEALTH UNIVERSITY

FAIRCHILD PUBLICATIONS, INC.

NEW YORK

EXECUTIVE EDITOR: Olga T. Kontzias
ACQUISITIONS EDITOR: Joseph Miranda
ASSISTANT ACQUISITIONS EDITOR: Jaclyn Bergeron
ART DIRECTOR: Adam B. Bohannon
PRODUCTION MANAGER: Ginger Hillman
SENIOR DEVELOPMENT EDITOR: Amy Zarkos
ASSOCIATE PRODUCTION EDITOR: Beth Cohen
COPY EDITOR: Annie McDonnell
TEXT DESIGN AND LAYOUT: Sara E. Stemen
COVER DESIGN: Sara E. Stemen
CD-ROM DEVELOPER: Adam B. Bohannon
CD-ROM MANUFACTURER: Rainbow Multimedia Inc.

Copyright © 2006 Fairchild Publications, Inc.

All rights reserved. No part of this book covered by the copyright hereon may be reproduced or used in any form or by any means-graphic, electronic, or mechanical, including photocopying, recording, taping, or information storage and retrieval systems-without written permission of the publisher.

LIBRARY OF CONGRESS CATALOG CARD NUMBER: 2005937933

ISBN: 1-56367-377-0

GST R 133004424

PRINTED IN THE UNITED STATES OF AMERICA

TP08, CM01

Contents

Extended Contents

Preface

Perry's Department Store: A Product Development Simulation, the second textbook of a series of merchandising simulations, bridges the gap between theory and principles of fashion product development and the actual process of developing a line of apparel for the fashion industry. It has been the authors' experience that students have difficulty applying concepts and theories to real world experiences.

The highest level of learning comes from the application of new knowledge to similar but different situations. Students are often uncomfortable with a learning environment or problem that doesn't exactly replicate models or examples of solutions. However, the world of work requires that students do exactly this: solve new problems with current knowledge, research (new knowledge), and experience. Hence, this simulation requires that students use problem solving and research to formulate new answers to new problems. There is not one right answer to any of the steps of this simulation: What is important is how well the student can support the decisions made with research, application of principles and theories, and merchandising knowledge.

This simulation is organized into eleven chapters, with seven of the chapters representing steps that replicate the process that most organizations employ to develop apparel lines. Each chapter begins with the introduction of concepts and merchandising information to be used in the simulation part of the text. The simulation or assignment follows, telling students what to do next; however, as with any work assignment, there are many ways to interpret the information provided that produce many different results.

The text begins with background information about Perry's, a fictitious department store, so that students have a basis to begin their research and start formulating a sense of their employer and market. Step One provides data about Perry's customers and is merely a beginning or launching point for student research. As would any competent buyer or product developer, students must define their customer, their new market, and the trends impacting that market (Step Two). This textbook provides demographics and psychographics, but this information should be continually reviewed and updated. Today's Internet sources provide a wealth of information about people, product, and trends, and are a great resource for students completing this simulation.

Once students become current on their customer and market, they can begin the creative elements of defining product themes and inspiration (Step Three) and actually conceptualizing their product line (Step Four). Step Five requires that students choose the best fabrication, findings, and trim for their line while considering pricing, availability, and sourcing constraints. Step Six of this simulation calls for students to clearly communicate the specifications of their product line, introducing them to specification sheets and the technical elements of product development. The final step, Step Seven, walks students through the completion of the spec pack, including size specifications, cost sheets, and the importance of accuracy in production patterns, grading, and marker making.

Chapters Nine and Ten address what happens after the line has been developed, including production issues, quality control and assurance, and marketing and public relations. Chapter Eleven overviews careers in product development from both a retail and wholesale perspective.

Accompanying the text is a CD-ROM that provides additional resources for the students to use while completing this simulation. All the necessary forms and worksheets are included on the CD-ROM as well as customer data, industry reports, examples of theme and concept boards, and other resources.

This simulation was developed to replicate the product development process, but because of the complexity of the process, the authors attempted to simplify some of the steps while maintaining its authenticity. Not all organizations develop products the same way, so the simulation represents a compilation of many methods while using those that appear to be the most commonly seen in the fashion industry. For example, a retail organization the size of Perry's could not afford to develop a private-label line of jeans in such small quantities and still make a competitive product that could produce gross margin results worthy of the company's efforts. The authors felt, however, that a smaller store with smaller quantities would be less overwhelming to students and still represent the process of product development.

The most significant feature of the text and CD-ROM is their ability to replicate the real-life experience for students, so they can better understand the product development process and the role of the merchandiser/buyer in the process. Today's business environment requires employees to solve problems, research new information, and exercise informed decision-making skills. There is an element of risk taking in developing concepts and applying new information that makes students uncomfortable. However, this experience will only enrich their ability to cope in a contemporary work environment that requires employees to think and solve problems. The nature of the simulation requires *students* to remain up-to-date with the business environment by researching current information about the industry, the customer, and the trends; this prevents the text from becoming dated.

The Instructor's Guide is available to assist faculty with teaching suggestions, alternative viewpoints, and examples of what the completed student simulation might look like. The authors understand the textbook will be used differently by every faculty member and have provided viable suggestions on how faculty might use the resources and simulation to improve student learning.

Acknowledgments

A simulation requires professional information, expertise, and access to privileged information, and the authors would like to express their gratitude to the numerous individuals and organizations that assisted them in this endeavor. They would like to acknowledge the following individuals: Bob Videtic, senior vice president, S & K Famous Brands; Pat Breman, SRI Consulting Business Intelligence; Carrie L. Hollenberg, senior consultant, SRI Consulting Business Intelligence; Rita Nakouzi, trend analyst, Promostyl; Russell Seymour, vice president, Fredericksburg Regional Alliance; Noelle McKown, adjunct faculty, Virginia Commonwealth University, Department of Fashion; Jeff Koss and Michael Silverman; What's Hot Apparel Group; Donna Reamy, assistant chairperson, Virginia Commonwealth University, Department of Fashion; Cindi Steele, vice president of product development, Evergreen Enterprises; Ken Farah, president, Pearl River Textiles; Maria DiClemente, vice president, and Elaine Guirleo, product coordinator, of Milco Industries; George Kress, president of Character, Inc.; Jaz Conlon, vice president of Kenneth Cole Productions; Nate Herman, international trade advisor, American Apparel & Footwear Association; and Chip Berry, Cone Mills.

Reviewers selected by the publisher were also very helpful. They include Richard Clodfelter, University of South Carolina; Cynthia Jasper, University of Wisconsin; Sharon Pate, Illinois State University; and Susan Stark, San Francisco State University.

CHAPTER 1

INTRODUCTION

Perry's Background Information

IN THIS CHAPTER, YOU WILL LEARN:

* The term *simulation* and how it is used in this textbook
* Statistical and demographic information needed to develop product for a specific customer or market
* Statistical information to define a customer base and that customer's product wants and needs
* The breadth of a buyer's job as it relates to product development

This chapter explains the simulation aspect of this textbook and introduces a fictitious regional department store that has a downtown flagship store and four branch stores. The store interior, sales volume, and customer profile are different for each branch based on a standardized customer assortment that has been developed by the buyer for each department. The buyer has been asked to develop a new product line of denim **jeans** to be introduced into the branded assortment of jeans that is already carried. Based on demographic, psychographic, and industry research, the student will develop a customer profile for each store assortment. They will learn about market segmentation, industry knowledge, and the development of a step-by-step plan to bring their products to market at Perry's.

It should be acknowledged that a department store the size of Perry's would not develop product on a **private-label** basis because of the size of its operation. Private-label products are developed to create exclusivity and increase **gross margin** numbers, and are based on economies of scale. The more products that are manufactured, the less expensive the unit cost; however, the number of units produced must be significant if the process is to be cost-effective. The number of units produced varies with the type of product and the development costs of that item; however, the exact number is usually determined by the manufacturer or factory as a "minimum" order standard. This minimum purchase could vary from 1,000 units to 10,000 units depending on the type of merchandise. This simulation recognizes that Perry's is too small an operation to be involved in developing private-label lines, but for the sake of learning, the simulation maintains that the process is the same; just the numbers are smaller to make the examples less overwhelming.

OBJECTIVES OF THE SIMULATION

After completing the simulation, students will be able to:

* Understand the breadth of the buyer's responsibilities with regard to product development and buying in a retail organization

* Research market trends, industry trends, demographics, and psychographics

* Understand the product development process

* Create theme, inspiration, and design concept boards

* Evaluate cost, availability, performance, and sourcing options

* Understand the impact of *quotas* and time constraints on the process

* Develop specification sheets and costing sheets

* Discuss the preproduction and production process and the inherent problems that inhibit apparel production

* Develop a sales plan and *marketing* plan for a new product line

THE SIMULATION: WHAT IS IT AND HOW DOES IT WORK?

A simulation can be defined as a similar situation, resembling but not exactly like the conditions that exist in reality. For the sake of this simulation, you will be provided with basic statistical and demographic information necessary to make product development and buying decisions. It will be your responsibility to research other sources of information to substantiate your design and product decisions and assist you in providing a basis for logical decision making based on actual industry and market trends.

Perry's is fictitious, as is the statistical store information, and is in no way representative of any specific retail organization.

FIGURE 01.01

Regional map of Fredericksburg, Virginia.

SOURCE: Courtesy of the Fredericksburg Regional Alliance

PERRY'S DEMOGRAPHIC INFORMATION

Perry's is a small, suburban department store located in Fredericksburg, Virginia (Figure 01.01). Its flagship store is located in the historic downtown area of the city of Fredericksburg, and its four branch operations surround the city, located in local shopping malls within a 40-mile radius of downtown.

Fredericksburg is located approximately 45 miles south of Washington, D.C., and is 45 miles north of Richmond, Virginia, the state capital. It is fast becoming what is called a "bedroom community" of the Washington area, with almost 50 percent of the residents commuting to D.C. for work each day. Presently there is a commuter train system that connects Union Station in Washington with downtown Fredericksburg.

As is much of Virginia, Fredericksburg is important in southern history, and it offers several historical tourist sites, including the boyhood home of George Washington and the location of four significant battles in the Civil War. Fredericksburg is also the home of University of Mary Washington, a four-year liberal arts institution.

There are a total of five Perry's stores, with one downtown Fredericksburg flagship store and four branch operations that are located in counties that surround the city of

Fredericksburg: Stafford, Caroline, and Spotsylvania. One store is located in Dale City in Prince William County. Changing demographics reflect the growth of the commuter population. The median home value for the Fredericksburg metropolitan area is $135,800 (2000) as compared to $262,000 in the Washington, D.C., region. The cost of living ERI index is 105.9 as compared to D.C.'s 137.4, making Fredericksburg an attractive alternative to the Washington area (www.simplyfredericksburg.com/fredericksburg/regional.shtml).

The Fredericksburg Regional Alliance reports, "The workforce in the Fredericksburg region boasts educational attainment levels that surpass the national average and that have been on a steady rise throughout the decade. This is due in part to the kind of people who move to the region: Over twice as many have bachelor degrees as the national average—they even outrank those in the Washington, D.C., metro area." The

TABLE 01.01

POPULATION GROWTH

	2000 POPULATION	2001 POPULATION	POPULATION GROWTH 2000-2001	ESTIMATED POPULATION GROWTH PER YEAR	% DIFFERENCE
VIRGINIA	7,078,515	7,187,734	109,219	65,908	+ 19.4
REGION	241,044	257,186	16,142	6,576	+ 59.3
CITY OF FREDERICKSBURG	19,279	19,952	673	542	+ 19.4
CAROLINE COUNTY	22,121	22,463	342	298	+ 12.9
SPOTSYLVANIA COUNTY	90,395	97,760	7,365	2,060	+ 73.2
DALE CITY	55,971	Not available	Not available	Not available	Not available
STAFFORD COUNTY	92,446	99,692	7,246	3,155	+ 56.5

SOURCE: Courtesy of the Fredericksburg Regional Alliance (www.fra-yes.org/datafile/population.htm) and U.S. Census Bureau

TABLE 01.02

WORKFORCE SURVEY
FREDERICKSBURG REGION: DISTRIBUTION OF WHITE-COLLAR WORKERS

OCCUPATION	RESIDENTS WORKING IN THE FREDERICKSBURG REGION	OUT COMMUTERS	ALL RESIDENTS
PROFESSIONAL	28%	33%	31%
EXECUTIVE	18	23	21
SALES & MARKETING	13	5	9
TECHNICIAN	6	7	6
OFFICE SUPPORT	14	13	13
TOTAL	79	81	80

SOURCE: Courtesy of the Fredericksburg Regional Alliance (www.fra-yes.org/datafile/population.htm)

region has an annual population growth of 4 percent with a workforce of 75,000 and an additional 909,000 workers within a 40-mile commute zone (Table 01.01) (www.fra-yes.org/workforce.htm).

The region's commuters, about 48 percent of the employed workforce, work primarily in Richmond, northern Virginia, and Washington, D.C. There is a well-educated workforce of approximately 30,000 persons with key occupational skills including (Table 01.02):

* 11,800 professionals (engineers, computer programmers, systems analysts, scientists, and medical professionals)

* 8,000 executives, managers, and administrators

* 4,500 office support personnel, including administrative, clerical, and customer

* 2,500 technicians and others

TABLE 01.03

MEDIAN AGE

	1990	2000
REGION	30.8	34.1
CITY OF FREDERICKSBURG	28.8	30.3
STAFFORD COUNTY	29.9	33.1
SPOTSYLVANIA COUNTY	30.8	34.3
CAROLINE COUNTY	33.	37.7

SOURCE: Courtesy of the Fredericksburg Regional Alliance (www.fra-yes.org/datafile/population.htm) and U.S. Census Bureau

TABLE 01.04

AGE GROUPS AS PERCENTAGE OF TOTAL POPULATION

	UNDER 5	UNDER 18	18 TO 64	OVER 64
REGION	7.0%	26.4%	56.7%	9.9%
CITY OF FREDERICKSBURG	5.8	17.8	63.6	12.8
CAROLINE COUNTY	6.2	24.8	56.1	12.9
SPOTSYLVANIA COUNTY	7.6	30.0	54.1	8.3
DALE CITY	8.1	27.5	61.2	3.2
STAFFORD COUNTY	7.8	31.6	54.7	5.9

SOURCE: Courtesy of the Fredericksburg Regional Alliance (www.fra-yes.org/datafile/population.htm) and U.S. Census Bureau

TABLE 01.05

MEDIAN HOUSEHOLD INCOME

	1989		1999		1989–1999	
	HOUSEHOLDS	MEDIAN INCOME*	HOUSEHOLDS	MEDIAN INCOME	HOUSEHOLD GROWTH	MEDIAN INCOME GROWTH
CITY OF FREDERICKSBURG	7,469	$26,614	8,086	$34,585	8.3%	30.0%
CAROLINE COUNTY	6,588	28,934	8,025	39,845	21.8	37.7
SPOTSYLVANIA COUNTY	18,978	41,432	31,259	57,525	64.7	38.8
STAFFORD COUNTY	19,443	44,661	30,136	66,809	55.0	49.6

* 1989 Median Income not adjusted for inflation
SOURCE: Courtesy of the Fredericksburg Regional Alliance (www.fra-yes.org/datafile/housing.htm) and U.S. Census Bureau

The estimated population growth for the Fredericksburg region exceeds the state of Virginia, with Stafford County estimated at a 34.1 percent growth rate between 2001 and 2010; the city of Fredericksburg is 28.1 percent; Spotsylvania is 22.8 percent; and Caroline County's growth rate is estimated at 13.5 percent. The population of the Fredericksburg region is expected to increase by 27.3 percent between 2001 and 2010 (www.fra-yes.org/datafile/population.htm).

The population of the Fredericksburg region is also maturing, with the median age for the area increasing from 30.8 to 34.1 in the last ten years (Table 01.03). The population distribution reveals that more than 66 percent of the residents in the region are over 18 years old, with 33 percent of the population being under 18 years old (Table 01.04). The region is very family-oriented, with not only a significant growth in population but also a growth in median household income. In the past ten years, the area has seen between a 30 percent and 49 percent growth in median income (Table 01.05). The area is quickly becoming relatively cosmopolitan compared to its rural beginnings (www.fra-yes.org/datafile/population.htm).

Perry's classifies its branch stores by ranking them either as an A, B, or C store according to their sales volume and the customer profile of the average customer who patronizes each branch. Most large retailers (department stores and chain stores) rank stores so that they can establish the best assortment of styles and merchandise to fit the customer profile of each branch. The ranking system may use letters of the alphabet (A, B, C, D) or numerals (I, II, III, IV). The ranking system is based not only on sales volume and customer profile but also on the following:

* Square footage of department

* Interior decor and fixtures

* Inventory levels

* Stock assortment (broad and shallow or narrow and deep)

* Price assortment

* Progressive attitude with regard to fashion purchases

* Store personnel

"A" stores have the largest square footage, with high sales volume, fashion-forward merchandise, and a higher average purchase. The merchandise assortment probably includes designer merchandise that is on the introduction stage of the fashion cycle and with a broad and shallow assortment. This means that there are many different styles (broad) with a limited number of sizes and colors (shallow) carried in the individual department assortments. Generally customers who purchase at the introduction stage of the fashion cycle want merchandise that is relatively exclusive based on availability and price. Buyers would choose merchandise that would meet these criteria: designer merchandise at high prices and the assortment limited to maybe only three or four different sizes and one color of a style. This customer doesn't want to see everyone else wearing what she has just purchased (exclusivity).

"B" stores have lower sales volume and inventory levels, with a decrease in the average purchase. The customer tends to be higher on the fashion cycle, in the acceptance stage, being more price-sensitive and less concerned with appearing on the cutting edge of fashion. The retail buyer's assortment would reflect this customer by searching out knockoffs from the Paris runway or designer fashions that would represent proven styles but at a lower price point and carried in a deeper assortment (more sizes and colors).

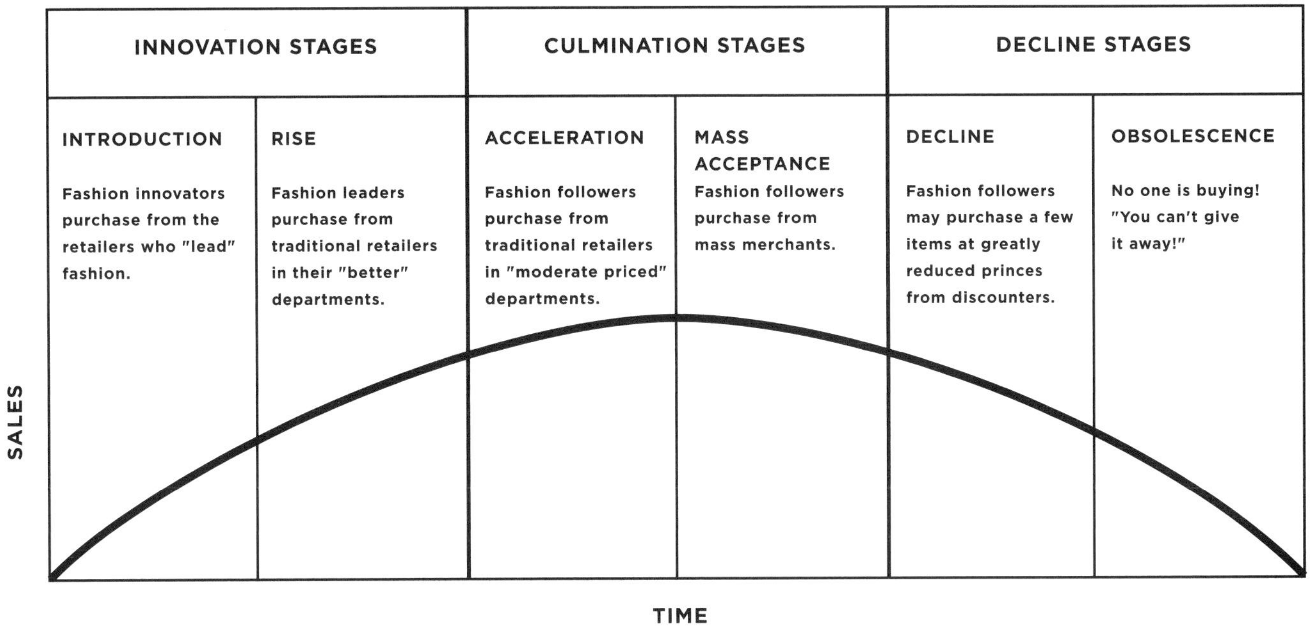

INNOVATION STAGES		CULMINATION STAGES		DECLINE STAGES	
INTRODUCTION Fashion innovators purchase from the retailers who "lead" fashion.	**RISE** Fashion leaders purchase from traditional retailers in their "better" departments.	**ACCELERATION** Fashion followers purchase from traditional retailers in "moderate priced" departments.	**MASS ACCEPTANCE** Fashion followers purchase from mass merchants.	**DECLINE** Fashion followers may purchase a few items at greatly reduced princes from discounters.	**OBSOLESCENCE** No one is buying! "You can't give it away!"

SALES

TIME

FIGURE 01.02 *The fashion cycle*

"C" stores have the lowest sales volume, the least progressive consumers with regard to fashion attitude, and their customers are the most price-sensitive. They are concerned with value over styling and would enter the fashion cycle on the culmination stage of the fashion cycle, where similar products are available widely and at declining costs to the consumer. Knockoffs abound at this stage of the fashion cycle, and similar styles are seen off price and in discount stores. This is fashion for the masses.

Figure 01.02 shows the fashion cycle representing the "sales life" of a fashion item. The fashion cycle explains the acceptance and the later rejection of styles over a period of time. This bell-shaped curve addresses the five stages of consumer acceptance and defines each stage with regard to style innovation, customer attitude, cost of the garment, and depth and breadth of assortment.

The first stages of this cycle, *innovation*, represent new styles that are high-priced, produced in very limited amounts, and targeted to a fashion "leader." This merchandise is often hot off the runways of Paris and New York and is tested for acceptance by the retail buyer. The substage, *introduction*, is represented by couture and designer merchandise that is bought in limited quantities and marketed heavily through fashion shows, institutional advertising, and designer appearances. As merchandise is accepted by a larger group of consumers, it moves to the *rise* substage. Merchandise in this sub-

TABLE 01.06

TOTAL SALES BY STORE AND FASHION CYCLE

STORE CLASSIFICATION	LOCATION	SALES VOLUME	PERCENT OF TOTAL	FASHION CYCLE
A STORE	Downtown	$13,650,000	27.3	Late Introduction
A STORE	Spotsylvania	13,200,000	26.4	Late Introduction
B STORE	Dale City	9,550,000	19.1	Early Rise
B STORE	Stafford	9,100,000	18.2	Rise
C STORE	Caroline	4,500,000	9.0	Culmination
TOTAL		50,000,000	100.0	

stage has been adapted or "knocked off" from the styles found in the first substage. Larger quantities are produced and the price of the garment drops (Stone, p.10).

The next stages, *culmination,* represent merchandise that is at the peak of its popularity and acceptance. It is readily available to the masses and is found at numerous different price points. Mass production, less expensive fabrication, and imported line-for-line copies make these styles affordable for a fashion-conscious consumer who either cannot afford the merchandise of the innovation stages or is unwilling to take the fashion risk of being the first to wear a new style. Consumers and buyers of merchandise at the innovation stages will no longer purchase merchandise that has moved into the culmination stage. To the innovation customer, it has become passé (Stone, pp.11-13).

The *acceleration* substage of the culmination stage consists of fashion followers who purchase moderate-price merchandise and shop at traditional retailers, especially department stores. Private-label merchandise is often targeted to this customer. The *mass acceptance* substage consumer frequents large national discount retailers for styles that are readily accepted and widely available (Stone, p.13).

Consumers crave new styles and once they become bored with a look, the merchandise moves into the *decline* stages. This is the substage of decline where items are deeply discounted and are often promoted as "Clearance." Customers will continue to wear the style but they will no longer buy any additional items. Production has stopped and merchandise is marked down. Leading stores no longer carry the merchandise but it will still appear at closeout prices in bargain stores. When merchandise can no longer be sold at any price, it reaches the substage of *obsolescence*. It will only be found in thrift shops and/or as recycled rags (Stone, p.13).

Table 01.06 ranks Perry's branch stores according to sales volume and how the majority of the customers appear on the fashion cycle.

PERRY'S: A TRADITIONAL MODEL FOR TODAY'S DEPARTMENT STORE

Perry's is a traditional department store with merchandise planning and control resting in the hands of a departmental buyer who is responsible for a specialized category of merchandise sold in the store. Each buyer is expected to be an authority on his or her department, including but not limited to the following:

* Development of a six-month plan

* Development of the model assortment plan

* Trend and market analysis

* Vendor analysis

* Supervision of assistant buyers

* Development of long-range department plans and goals

* Accurate recording of all transactions, including purchases, transfers, and returns to vendors, that affect the departmental inventory

* Promotional plans for the department

* Communication with store managers, departmental sales managers, and departmental sales personnel

* Communication with divisional merchandise manager

* Selection of merchandise to meet customer base, including the development of new private-label product lines, and the delivery of those goods

* Knowledge of import regulations, quotas, and successful delivery of privately developed merchandise

Perry's executive management has chosen you to develop and test-market a new private line of denim jeans in your department. They are confident that you can achieve a desirable gross margin, capture a new niche for your department, and increase classification sales. For the purpose of this simulation, you will select one of the following departments: Childrens, Juniors, Mens, or Misses.

Your step-by-step plan is as follows:

STEP I	Define the customer who shops at Perry's and for whom you will develop product (denim jeans)
STEP II	Conduct research on market and fashion trends in your department and about your denim product
STEP III	Develop theme and inspiration boards representing initial concepts for your product line
STEP IV	Create design boards, including illustrations, fabrication, color/treatment, and sales plan
STEP V	Choose fabrication, *findings* and *trim* and research countries of origin, including quotas, availability, and cost
STEP VI	Develop specification sheets or a blueprint for your product
STEP VII	Develop costing sheets
STEP VIII	Review the preproduction and production process, including sourcing and *quality control*
STEP IX	Develop a sales and marketing plan, and include public relations opportunities

There are guidelines for each step of your plan that will be revealed to you as you complete this simulation. Remember that you must justify in writing all of your product decisions, as upper management is scrutinizing you. Your justifications should include the citing of outside sources, such as current articles, professional interviews, or any additional research that you have completed. There is not one right answer to this simulation; you will be evaluated on your research, analysis, and how well you support the decisions you made.

CHAPTER 2

STEP ONE

Define Your Customer

IN THIS CHAPTER, YOU WILL LEARN:

* How to analyze demographic and psychographic information to develop a consumer profile
* What publications and resources are available to fashion professionals

Your first assignment is to develop a customer profile for the private-label line of denim jeans you are going to produce for your department. Use the demographic and statistical information in Chapter 1, plus conduct some additional research in the area of psychographics. Psychographics explores the primary motivation for an individual's purchasing behaviors. In other words, why do we buy certain products and not others?

There are several marketing research organizations that provide psychographics. One of the most prestigious research companies, SRI International, was the first to develop an eight-segment framework that explains and predicts adult consumer behavior. This framework, now owned by SRI Consulting Business Intelligence, is called *VALS™ Psychology of Markets*. It was developed to explain the relationship between consumer behavior and psychology. Sidebar 02.01 explains the history and methodology of this research survey segmentation.

VALS has identified two dimensions to this behavioral framework: primary motivation and resources. An individual's primary motivation directs what they find meaningful in the world or about themselves. Consumers are moved to action by one of the three motivators: ideals, achievement, and self-expression. How an individual consumes resources and services is an extension of their personality. VALS believes that energy, self-confidence, intellectualism, novelty seeking, innovativeness, impulsiveness, leadership, and vanity play a critical role in consumption (www.sric-bi.com/VALS/types.shtml). Sidebar 02.02 explains the two dimensions in more depth.

History and Methodology

VALS™ pioneered the quest for greater consumer understanding.

Arnold Mitchell was a consumer futurist who wanted to explain the fragmentation of U.S. society in the 1960s and the implications for the economy and society. His work led to the development of the original VALS™ system as a model to explain various attitudes toward society and institutions. This work drew the attention of visionary marketers who encouraged Mitchell to enhance and extend his work as a marketing tool. SRI International formally inaugurated the VALS program in 1978, which led to a 1983 best-selling book, *Nine American Lifestyles. Advertising Age* cited VALS as "one of the ten top market research breakthroughs of the 1980s." Mitchell's pioneering method of applying psychographics to business management and marketing research led marketers to become interested in VALS as a way of thinking of consumers beyond demographics.

VALS™ evolved to explain the relationship between psychology and consumer behavior.

In the late 1980s the original VALS system's ability to predict consumer behavior was weakening as attitudes evolved. The VALS team realized that it should make improvements. From 1986 to 1989, the team built a new system to maximize the ability to predict consumer behavior using psychology as a more stable platform. A team from SRI International, Stanford University, and the University of California, Berkeley, determined that individual differences affect purchase behavior more directly than do societal trends and that consumer personality dimensions are more stable over time than shared values and beliefs.

A new VALS system emerged. Still grounded in the philosophy that mind-set and demographics are more powerful than demographics alone, VALS now uses psychology to describe the dynamics underlying consumer preferences and choices.

The current VALS system also incorporates a resource dimension and focuses less on social maturation than did the original system. Consumers are constrained in their full expression of self through behavior and purchase. So VALS also measures a person's ability to express himself or herself in the marketplace.

VALS™ identifies the psychological motivations that predict consumer differences.

The foundation of the VALS approach is that behavior is controlled by relatively independent psychological traits. VALS uses proprietary psychometric techniques to measure concepts that researchers have proved empirically to correlate with consumer behavior. The inherent stability of the system 15 years after its development is testimony to the theories of the development team.

SOURCE: VALS™ Program. SRI Consulting Business Intelligence. http://www.sric-bi.com/vals

SIDEBAR 02.01

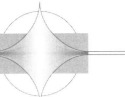 

The Framework

Motivations and resources determine how a person will express himself or herself in the marketplace.

People buy products and services and seek experiences that fulfill their characteristic preferences and give shape, substance, and satisfaction to their lives. An individual's primary motivation determines what in particular about the self or the world is the meaningful core that governs his or her activities. VALS™ isolates the patterns that reinforce and sustain a person's identity as the person expresses it in the marketplace.

Some consumers choose what is "best."

Individuals motivated by *ideals* are grounded in knowledge and principles. For some people, this motivation is manifest in intellectual curiosity and quiet philosophical searching. For others, it expresses in an adherence to a personal or social code of conduct, such as religious, moral, or ethical convictions. In either case, the tendency is to base decisions on abstract, idealized criteria such as quality, integrity, and tradition.

Others are motivated by symbols of success.

People who are motivated by *achievement* strive for a clear social position. They seek explicit responsibilities and approval from a valued social group. Their focus is often on collective activities, such as those at work and with family, and on positive evaluation and reward. They base their choices on the expected reactions, concerns, and desires of people in the groups to which they belong or aspire to belong.

And some are driven by experience.

Individuals motivated by *self-expression* value actions for their impact on the physical world or the pleasure and excitement associated with them. A vital, emotional attachment to experiences is typical of this primary motivation, as is resistance to social controls that threaten experimentation and self-reliance. These action-oriented consumers make choices that emphasize individuality and personal challenge.

Psychological attributes strongly influence a person's ability and desire to buy.

A person's tendency to consume goods and services extends beyond age, income, and education. Energy, self-confidence, intellectualism, novelty seeking, innovativeness, impulsiveness, leadership, and vanity play a critical role. These personality traits in conjunction with key demographics determine an individual's resources. Different levels of resources enhance or constrain a person's expression of his or her primary motivation. The resource dimension gives VALS a hierarchical design, with the segments at the top of the map having a greater impact in the marketplace.

SOURCE: VALS™ Program. SRI Consulting Business Intelligence. http://www.sric-bi.com/vals

SIDEBAR 02.02

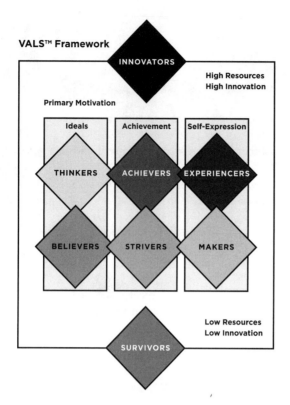

VALS™ Framework

INNOVATORS

High Resources
High Innovation

Primary Motivation

| Ideals | Achievement | Self-Expression |

THINKERS   ACHIEVERS   EXPERIENCERS

BELIEVERS   STRIVERS   MAKERS

Low Resources
Low Innovation

SURVIVORS

FIGURE 02.01

Eight segments of VALS™

SOURCE: VALS™ Program. SRI Consulting
Business Intelligence. www.sric-bi.com/vals

THE SEGMENTS

VALS™ segments the U. S. English-speaking population age 18 or older into eight consumer groups. Their primary motivation and ability to express themselves in the marketplace distinguish the groups.

Innovators
Innovators are successful, sophisticated, take-charge people with high self-esteem. Because they have such abundant resources, they exhibit all three primary motivations in varying degrees. They are change leaders and are the most receptive to new ideas and technologies. Their purchases reflect cultivated tastes for upscale, niche products and services.

Thinkers   Motivated by ideals; high resources
Thinkers are mature, satisfied, comfortable, and reflective. They tend to be well educated and actively seek out information in the decision-making process. They favor durability, functionality, and value in products.

Believers   Motivated by ideals; low resources
Believers are strongly traditional and respect rules and authority. Because they are fundamentally conservative, they are slow to change and technology averse. They choose familiar products and established brands.

Achievers   Motivated by achievement; high resources
Achievers have goal-oriented lifestyles that center on family and career. They avoid situations that encourage a high degree of stimulation or change. They prefer premium products that demonstrate success to their peers.

Strivers   Motivated by achievement; low resources
Strivers are trendy and fun loving. They have little discretionary income and tend to have narrow interests. They favor stylish products that emulate the purchases of people with greater material wealth.

Experiencers   Motivated by self-expression; high resources
Experiencers appreciate the unconventional. They are active and impulsive, seeking stimulation from the new, offbeat, and risky. They spend a comparatively high proportion of their income on fashion, socializing, and entertainment.

Makers   Motivated by self-expression; low resources
Makers value practicality and self-sufficiency. They choose hands-on constructive activities and spend leisure time with family and close friends. Because they prefer value to luxury, they buy basic products.

Survivors
Survivors lead narrowly focused lives. Because they have the fewest resources, they do not exhibit a primary motivation and often feel powerless. They are primarily concerned about safety and security, so they tend to be brand loyal and buy discounted merchandise.

VALS studies individuals to measure their underlying psychological motivations and examine the resources that these individuals have in common. The VALS survey predicts each group's typical choices as consumers and believes that people "express their personalities through their behavior." VALS defines consumer segments based on those personality traits that affect behavior in the marketplace. VALS uses psychology to segment people according to their distinct personality traits rather than looking at what people do and activities they enjoy. The personality traits are the motivation—the cause. "Buying behavior becomes the effect—the observable, external behavior prompted by an internal driver (www.sric-bi.com/VALS/types.shtml)."

Figure 02.01 provides a visual introduction to the eight VALS segments: Innovators, Thinkers, Achievers, Experiencers, Believers, Strivers, Makers, and Survivors. Within this figure, you will also find descriptions of each segment. Innovators are sophisticated consumers with take-charge attitudes. They are resource-laden and very open to new ideas and products. Thinkers are motivated by ideals and are considered by VALS to be "satisfied, mature, comfortable, and reflective people that value order, knowledge, and responsibility." According to VALS, Achievers are goal-oriented with a strong commitment to family and career. Politically conservative, value conscious, and with respect for authority, Achievers lead relatively conventional lives. Experiencers are motivated by self-expression, enjoying new and offbeat items or services. They are avid consumers of fashion, focusing on "looking good." Believers are motivated by ideals with conservative and traditional values. They tend to buy "Made in the USA" and are loyal consumers. Strivers are trendy, fun-loving individuals who seek the approval of others. They prefer stylish items and emulate people who are better off financially. Makers are also self-expressive individuals who are practical and value self-sufficiency. They tend to be unimpressed with material possessions and prefer value to luxury. And finally, Survivors are cautious consumers because of their limited resources. They prefer the familiar and attempt to meet just the most basic needs. Go to www.sric-bi.com/VALS/, and take the VALS survey to determine your VALS type. Your individual profile should help you understand how psychographics are used to determine consumer behavior.

VALS, in conjunction with Mediamark Research Inc., has provided you with additional market research on the consumption of denim jeans in Table 02.01 and Part II of the CD-ROM. This table provides data on the number of jeans purchased and the amount spent on jeans for both men and women by VALS segments. Sidebar 02.03 provides you with instructions on how to read the data.

DATA TO SELECT A TARGET FOR JEANS

		All	Innovator	Thinker	Believer	Achiever	Striver	Experiencer	Maker	Survivor
Total U.S.	Unwgtd	26797	2440	5354	4307	6283	2190	1646	1893	2684
	'(OOO)	205368	20536	23213	33886	29169	23615	26077	24230	24642
	Horz %	100	10	11.3	16.5	14.2	11.5	12.7	11.8	12
	Vert %	100	100	100	100	100	100	100	100	100
	Index	100	100	100	100	100	100	100	100	100

BOUGHT IN THE LAST 12 MONTHS

		All	Innovator	Thinker	Believer	Achiever	Striver	Experiencer	Maker	Survivor
Bought Men's Jeans:	Unwgtd	6723	648	1233	866	1910	609	469	702	286
Any	'(OOO)	54997	5620	5644	7864	9076	6705	7692	9356	3040
	Horz %	100	10.22	10.26	14.3	16.5	12.19	13.99	17.01	5.53
	Vert %	26.78	27.37	24.31	23.21	31.11	28.39	29.5	38.62	12.34
	Index	100	102	91	87	116	106	110	144	46
Bought Men's Jeans:	Unwgtd	2950	166	430	430	851	324	225	399	125
3 or more pair	'(OOO)	26678	1574	2178	4054	4474	3690	3792	5481	1435
	Horz %	100	5.9	8.16	15.2	16.77	13.83	14.21	20.54	5.38
	Vert %	12.99	7.67	9.38	11.96	15.34	15.63	14.54	22.62	5.82
	Index	100	59	72	92	118	120	112	174	45
Bought Men's Jeans:	Unwgtd	4080	413	787	530	1132	355	227	434	202
Amount spent in total:	'(OOO)	32873	3572	3594	4654	5313	3933	3889	5727	2190
Under $50	Horz %	100	10.87	10.93	14.16	16.16	11.96	11.83	17.42	6.66
	Vert %	16.01	17.39	15.48	13.73	18.22	16.65	14.91	23.64	8.89
	Index	100	109	97	86	114	104	93	148	56
Bought Men's Jeans:	Unwgtd	862	65	141	105	260	87	84	98	22
Amount spent in total:	'(OOO)	7533	630	692	1088	1364	906	1233	1375	246
Jeans: $100+	Horz %	100	8.36	9.18	14.44	18.1	12.02	16.37	18.25	3.26
	Vert %	3.67	3.07	2.98	3.21	4.68	3.83	4.73	5.67	1
	Index	100	84	81	88	127	105	129	155	27

TABLE 02.01

DATA TO SELECT A TARGET FOR JEANS

		All	Innovator	Thinker	Believer	Achiever	Striver	Experiencer	Maker	Survivor
BOUGHT IN THE LAST 12 MONTHS										
Bought Women's Jeans:	Unwgtd	5345	443	918	1022	1455	473	333	386	315
Any	'(000)	40963	4267	4340	7977	6935	4756	4800	5108	2780
	Horz %	100	10.42	10.6	19.47	16.93	11.61	11.72	12.47	6.79
	Vert %	19.95	20.78	18.7	23.54	23.78	20.14	18.41	21.08	11.28
	Index	100	104	94	118	119	101	92	106	57
Bought Women's Jeans:	Unwgtd	1897	111	259	423	483	193	149	164	115
3 or more pair	'(000)	15755	1133	1291	3369	2361	2019	2330	2253	998
	Horz %	100	7.19	8.2	21.38	14.99	12.82	14.79	14.3	6.34
	Vert %	7.67	5.52	5.56	9.94	8.1	8.55	8.93	9.3	4.05
	Index	100	72	73	130	106	111	116	121	53
Bought Women's Jeans:	Unwgtd	3467	284	607	672	919	314	167	271	233
Amount spent in total:	'(000)	26579	2742	2856	5131	4425	3228	2467	3618	2114
Jeans: Under $50	Horz %	100	10.32	10.74	19.3	16.65	12.14	9.28	13.61	7.95
	Vert %	12.94	13.35	12.3	15.14	15.17	13.67	9.46	14.93	8.58
	Index	100	103	95	117	117	106	73	115	66
Bought Women's Jeans:	Unwgtd	523	43	82	95	148	44	66	32	13
Amount spent in total:	'(000)	4327	443	417	818	781	450	926	393	97
Jeans: $100+	Horz %	100	10.25	9.65	18.91	18.05	10.41	21.41	9.08	2.24
	Vert %	2.11	2.16	1.8	2.41	2.68	1.91	3.55	1.62	0.39
	Index	100	102	85	115	127	91	169	77	19

SOURCE: VALS™/Mediamark Research Inc. 2003 doublebase. All rights reserved.

READING DATA TO SELECT
A TARGET CONSUMER FOR JEANS

Table 02.01 and the table on the attached CD-ROM contain national survey data about English-speaking U.S. adults, 18 years of age or older, who have purchased men's and women's jeans in the past 12 months. The data can point to a target for buyers of jeans. Reviewing all the numbers will produce the most accurate analysis.

The 11-column table contains data cross-tabulated by VALS™ segments from the VALS™/Mediamark Research Inc. 2003 doublebase data set. The questions asked of all survey respondents are in Column 1. Column 2 lists the abbreviated labels for the rows of numbers. Column 3 displays the numbers relating to all U.S. adults. Columns 4-11 show the numbers relating to each of the VALS segments.

The abbreviated labels are:

Unwgtd = *unweighted*
The numbers in this row show the actual number of people who participated in the survey or responded to the survey question.

In this example:

		All	Innovator	Thinker	Believer	Achiever	Striver	Experiencer	Maker	Survivor
Bought Men's Jeans Any	Unwgtd	6723	648	1233	866	1910	609	469	702	286

In the past 12 months 6,723 actual survey respondents bought at least one pair of men's jeans.

'(000) = the number of respondents in thousands
The numbers in this row show the weighted number of actual respondents projected to the total U.S. adult population.

In this example:

		All	Innovator	Thinker	Believer	Achiever	Striver	Experiencer	Maker	Survivor
Total U.S.	Unwgtd	26797	2440	5354	4307	6283	2190	1646	1893	2684
	'(000)	205368	20536	23213	33886	29169	23615	26077	24230	24642

The actual number of respondents, 26,797, projects to 205,368,000. Because the number listed in this row is displayed in thousands, always add 3 zeros to show the correct projected number.

Horz % = Horizontal percent
The Horz % row shows the *composition* of the consumer market who have purchased men's jeans in the past 12 months. The chart indicates the percentage of buyers who fall into each of the VALS segments—10.22% in the Innovator segment, for example.

		All	Innovator	Thinker	Believer	Achiever	Striver	Experiencer	Maker	Survivor
Bought Men's Jeans Any	Horz %	100	10.22	10.26	14.3	16.5	12.19	13.99	17.01	5.53

SIDEBAR 02.03

Vert % = Vertical percent
The numbers in the Vert % row show the ***penetration*** of jeans buying for the total population, as well as each VALS segment.

In this example:

		All	Innovator	Thinker	Believer	Achiever	Striver	Experiencer	Maker	Survivor
Bought Men's Jeans	Vert %	26.78	27.37	24.31	23.21	31.11	28.39	29.5	38,62	12.34
Any										

In the past 12 months 26.78% of all adults purchased men's jeans. This number is referred to as the ***base rate***. The chart shows that 27.37% of all Innovators bought men's jeans in the past 12 months, 31.11% of Achievers, 28.39% of Strivers, 29.5% of Experiencers, and so on.

Index
The numbers in the Index row represent the relationship between the vertical-percent numbers compared to the base rate.

In this example:

		All	Innovator	Thinker	Believer	Achiever	Striver	Experiencer	Maker	Survivor
Bought Men's Jeans	Vert %	12.99	7.67	9.38	11.96	15.34	15.63	14.54	22.62	5.82
3 or more pairs	Index	100	59	72	92	118	120	93	174	45

In the past 12 months 12.99% of all adults have purchased 3 or more pair of men's jeans—the base rate. An index of 59 means that the relationship between the instance of buying 3 or more pair of jeans among Innovators (7.67%) in relationship to the percentage of all adults having bought 3 or more pair of men's jeans in the past 12 months (12.99%), is below normal or average behavior, which is deemed to be 100.

Indices are a quick way to identify possible targets for consideration. For best results, read index numbers in ranges. Indices between 0-80 represent below-average behavior; 81-120 indicate average behavior; and 121 or more indicate above-average behavior. This method shows that only Makers (174) index above-average among adults who purchased 3 or more pair of men's jeans in the past 12 months.

But be aware that while indices are a fast way to visually scan data, they can be misleading. Often a low penetration of a segment can produce a high index. To select the correct target, it's best to carefully review all the numbers.

SOURCE: VALS™ Program. SRI Consulting Business Intelligence. http://www.sric-bi.com/vals

SIDEBAR 02.03

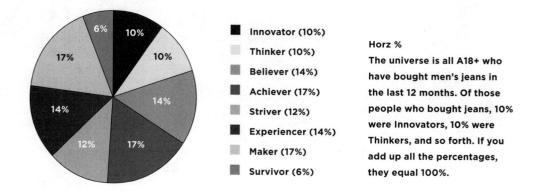

Innovator (10%)

Thinker (10%)

Believer (14%)

Achiever (17%)

Striver (12%)

Experiencer (14%)

Maker (17%)

Survivor (6%)

Horz %

The universe is all A18+ who have bought men's jeans in the last 12 months. Of those people who bought jeans, 10% were Innovators, 10% were Thinkers, and so forth. If you add up all the percentages, they equal 100%.

FIGURE 02.02

Horizontal percent of adults 18+ years old who have bought men's jeans in the last 12 months

SOURCE: VALS™/Mediamark Research Inc. 2003 doublebase.

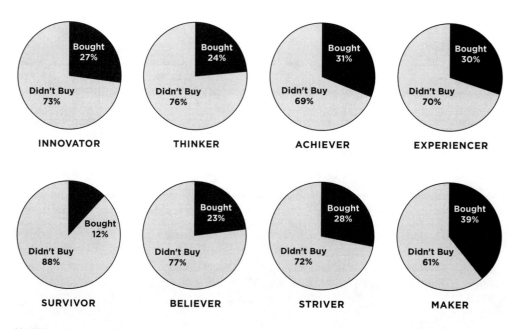

Vert %

Each VALS segment represents a different universe. For example, of Innovators, 27% bought men's jeans but 73% did not; those who bought and those who did not buy equal 100% of the Innovator universe.

FIGURE 02.03

Vertical percent of jeans purchased by each of the VALS™ segments

SOURCE: VALS™/Mediamark Research Inc. 2003 doublebase.

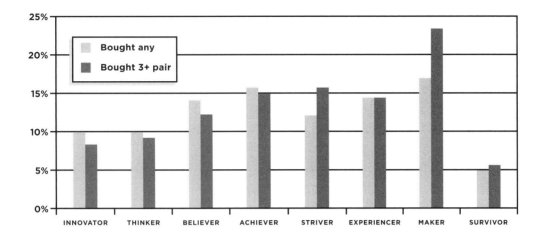

It's often helpful to visualize data by using charts. This chart shows the comparison between what percentage of each VALS segments bought any men's jeans last year and what percentage bought 3 pair or more. A data chart quickly shows that Makers are the heaviest men's jeans buyers.

FIGURE 02.04
Visualizing data
SOURCE: VALS™/Mediamark Research Inc. 2003 doublebase.

VALS has provided some visual interpretations of this data in Figure 02.02 through Figure 02.06. Figure 02.02 shows the horizontal percent defining all adults 18+ years old who have bought men's jeans in the last 12 months, distributed by VALS segments. The reason the table reflects all adults 18+ purchasing men's jeans rather than men 18+ is the fact that women purchase over half of all apparel for the men in their lives.

Figure 02.03 provides a visual interpretation of the vertical percent or the percentage of jeans purchased by each of the segments. Note the importance of not only the percentage that bought jeans but also the percentage of adults that didn't buy jeans in the last year.

Figure 02.04 visually compares by VALS segment the numbers of jeans purchased. Review of the data shows that Makers are the number one purchasers of jeans in this data.

Figure 02.05 is a visualization of the amount spent on jeans for men in the last 12 months. Makers bought the greatest numbers of jeans but spent the least on them (under $50.00) while Achievers and Experiencers spent the most (over $100.00) on their jeans. And finally, Figure 02.06 maps or plots the data on the VALS framework visually.

GeoVALS is another research tool and links the VALS segments to geographic locations throughout the United States by zip codes. It estimates the potential sales performance by location (zip codes), and can critique and define a merchandise mix based

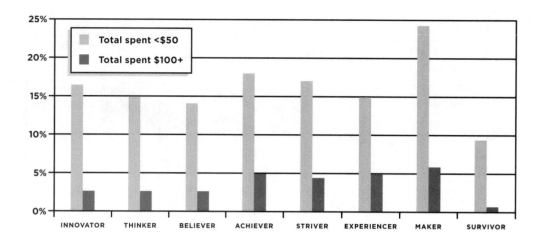

This chart shows the comparison between the percentage of each VALS segment's spending a total of $50 or less on all jeans purchased last year and what percentage spent $100 or more. This chart shows that Makers, closely followed by Achievers and Experiencers, are the most likely to have spent $100 or more on men's jeans in total last year.

FIGURE 02.05

Comparison of the percentage of each VALS™ segment's spending a total

SOURCE: VALS™/Mediamark Research Inc. 2003 doublebase.

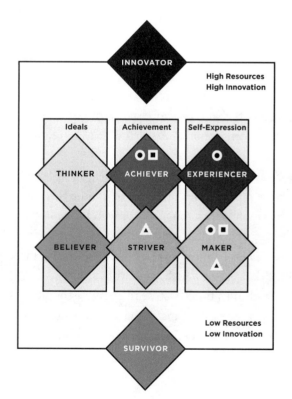

Another way to visualize data is to plot it on the VALS map. This method of visualizing data enables you to quickly spot the best target consumers. For example, Makers buy a lot of men's jeans and have spent more than $100 in the last 12 months on jeans. Understanding that Makers are practical Do-it-Yourselfers who value utility, not fashion, allows you to determine that they would be a good target for inexpensive work jeans.

■ Most likely to have bought men's jeans in the last 12 months

● Most likely to have spent $100 or more on men's jeans in the last 12 months

▲ Most likely to have bought 3 or more pair of men's jeans in the last 12 months

FIGURE 02.06

Map of jean purchases

SOURCE: © 2005 SRI Consulting Business Intelligence, VALS™. All rights reserved.

GEOVALS™ CAN TAKE YOU WHERE YOU NEED TO GO

Find the most important geography for your business

Fredericksburg, VA   **94,707 Adults 18+**

Innovators 12%	Strivers 9%
Thinkers 14%	Experiencers 15%
Believers 14%	Makers 11%
Achievers 19%	Survivors 6%

Analyzing geographic areas based on demographics alone or demographics combined with household behaviors have limited utility for marketers looking to increase their business by making emotional connections with their customers. Using the power of VALS™ to map your customers to geography, GeoVALS estimates the distribution of the eight VALS™ segments within all U.S. residential ZIP codes. GeoVALS enables users to find their best customers, or best potential customers for their products, services, site locations, and advertising. Find out where you need to go to increase your chance of success.

* **Market Potential**	Estimate the sales potential for your products or services based on the number of target consumers within your trade area.
* **Sales Analysis**	Analyze sales performace by region.
* **Site Location**	Select locations for retail outlets on the basis of concentrations of target customers.
* **Merchandise Mix**	Critique and refine merchandise mix given the consumers within a trading area.
* **Direct Marketing**	Increase hit rates by identifying those ZIP codes with the highest proportion of a target segment.
* **Media Analysis**	Tailor programming format and content to audience composition.

Sample GeoVALS™ ZIP-code data record

Data estimates are at the individual level—adults age 18 years or older. The GeoVALS data included on this CD is for Fredericksburg, VA.

Beginning with the specified ZIP code, the next eight columns show the proportion of each VALS segment followed by the number of adults age 18 or older in the ZIP.

Zip code	Innovators	Thinkers	Believers	Achievers	Strivers	Experiencers	Makers	Survivors	# of Adults	County	State
1	2	3	4	5	6	7	8	9	10	12	13
22427	4%	7%	23%	9%	11%	9%	15%	20%	1,997	Caroline	VA

FIGURE 02.07

GeoVALS™ data for Fredericksburg, Virginia

SOURCE: © 2005 SRI Consulting Business Intelligence, VALS™. All rights reserved.

_____ Store

Median Age:

Family Income:

Educational Level:

VALS™ and GeoVALS™ profile:

Competitive stores and brands within region:
(including private-label brands)

Fashion cycle emphasis:

Buying behaviors:

FIGURE 02.08   _Perry's consumer profile worksheet_

on concentrations of specific consumer segments. By combining VALS, Mediamark research data, and GeoVALS, product developers can create a powerful research tool to predict the wants and demands of consumers in any geographic location. For example only, GeoVALS locates a large number of Achievers living in the Fredericksburg area, and they know that Achievers have spent more than $100.00 on three or more pairs of denim jeans within the last year. Therefore, a buyer/product developer could predict that a market for jeans that cost over $50.00 exists in this market.

Figure 02.07 is a summary of the GeoVALS data for the Fredericksburg, Virginia, area and is an introduction to the data presented on the CD-ROM included with this textbook. You will find specific zip code data under GeoVALS Data for the Perry's Department Store Trading Area in Part II of the CD-ROM. You will also find a section titled VALS Applications in Part II, providing you with additional information on how this information can be used in product development and/or a retail environment.

There are also many other sources of information on who wears jeans, how much they are willing to pay for them, and what is important to the wearer. You must also consider the fact that the wearer and the purchaser are sometimes different people. Children wear jeans but their parents are the purchaser. You must consider both people in the product development process. You should use trade publications that are appropriate for your industry: *Daily News Record* (*DNR*) for men's wear; *Women's Wear Daily* (*WWD*) for women's wear and juniors; and *Children's Business* for children's and infant's clothing, to name a few publications that may offer you insight in defining your customer.

Upon completion of your research using VALS, any trade publication for your industry, or market research, create a customer profile for Perry's A and B store. Your profile should include the following information:

Median age
Family income
Educational level
VALS profile
Fashion cycle emphasis
Buying behaviors

Complete a worksheet for an A store, a B store, and a C store using the blank worksheet that is provided for you on the CD-ROM. Remember that you will have three separate worksheets, one for each ranking. An example of the consumer profile worksheet is shown in Figure 02.08.

SIMULATION:
Go to Figure 02.08 in the book or CD-ROM and to Part II on the CD-ROM.

CHAPTER 3

STEP TWO

Industry Research

IN THIS CHAPTER, YOU WILL LEARN:

* The types of information buyers and product developers use to design merchandise for their customer
* The resources used to research various fashion industries

Your next step in the product development process is to determine what your customer wants. You must know not only who your customer is (Step One) but what they like and dislike in a pair of jeans. You must understand market and fashion trends that will influence your customer's decision, and you must become an authority on your industry as quickly as possible. Your CD-ROM provides you with excellent sources of information as your starting point for your industry research. The research and articles can be found in Part III, the Industry Research portion of your CD-ROM, categorized by classification: Mens, Misses/Juniors, or Boys/Girls 4-7 or 4-6X. Remember that fashion is ever changing, and as a buyer/product developer you must be in tune with the pulse of the industry if you want to sell product and be successful.

The first part of your research should begin with your industry. Although the Misses market and the Junior market both cater to women, they are very different in many ways. Fashion often revolves around lifestyle and you must understand how your market's lifestyle influences their fashion choices. So the first part of your research should include the following general information for your segment of the fashion industry (men's, misses, junior, or children's):

* Scope and size of your segment of the fashion industry

* Age range

Calvin Klein Jeans Enters Premium Fray

Designer to introduce CK39 denim collection this week at MAGIC

By David Lipke

NEW YORK - A pricey new jeans label from Calvin Klein will debut this week at MAGIC, joining a crowded field of competitors jockeying for prominence in the premium denim market.

The new men's and women's line from Warnaco Group Inc.—which licenses the Calvin Klein name from Calvin Klein Inc., a subsidiary of Phillips Van-Heusen—is called CK39 and is aimed at upscale specialty and department stores. The company expects the label to roll out in 100 to 120 retail doors next spring.

"We knew we had an established Calvin Klein designer customer who was not able to purchase a pair of jeans from our existing offerings," said Colleen Kelly, president of Warnaco's Calvin Klein Jeans unit. "CK39 was designed with that customer in mind."

Tom Murry, president and chief operating officer of CKI, noted the initiative will allow Calvin Klein to target the premium/bridge segment of the market previously served by its CK Calvin Klein label (which has been reintroduced in the U.S. in women's, but not in men's). "The CK39 premium denim launch is the next step in solidifying the brand's position within this tier of business," he explained.

The spring men's collection from CK39 (the 39 refers to the Manhattan street where Calvin Klein's design studio is located) features jeans in four fits—boot, loose, classic and rocker—with retail prices from $145 to $225. In comparison, Warnaco's core Calvin Klein Jeans product is priced from $49 to $99.

Washes in the spring lineup include a lightweight resin-coated jean, dark dip ring-spun, sulphur-dyed black and porcelain ring-spun. "CK39 has very discreet design details in keeping with the Calvin Klein aesthetic," said Kelly. "It is not logo-driven, but rather based strictly on quality and luxury. The focus is not on overt wash details or about back pocket design, but about a true, clean wash."

Non-denim styles in the mix include high-luster stretch sateen jeans in a "rocker" fit, washed satin blazers, jean jackets, bombers, polo shirts and graphic-print T-shirts, all retailing from $65 to $265.

The label's offerings are distinguished by a gold hangtag with a simple, graphic CK39 logo. Jeans are embellished with a metal logo tag on a rear belt loop.

The spring launch will be supported with "a distinctive branding and marketing campaign, to be announced at a later date," said Kelly. "We will work with individual retailers to market the brand at a grassroots level," she added.

SOURCE: *Daily News Record*, August 30, 2004, p.18. Courtesy of Fairchild Publications, Inc.

SIDEBAR 03.01

* Size range

* Unique characteristics of your segment (i.e., purchaser vs. wearer, disposable income, frequency of shopping)

* Wholesale price points for jeans for your segment

* Expectations of this segment with regard to: quality, fabrication, fit, craftsmanship of jeans, labeling/branding

* Key brands and competitors' labels in the jean category of your segment

* Lifestyle of this customer within the segment

A few examples of this type of research are included on your CD-ROM under the Industry Research section and in Sidebar 03.01. Other useful articles might be found on Web sites such as www.just-style.com, which reported on Calvin Klein Jeans' unveiling of its premium denim line. The article explains that the new CK39 label is targeted to a luxury denim market for both men and women. The line will feature premium fabrication and finishes, gold satin-lined belt loops, and many additional features and details. The jeans will retail between $145 and $225. This type of article gives you insight as to the business decisions being made by key players in the jeans industry and provides specific product specifications for the premium jeans market. This information also could be useful to a buyer who was developing private-label jeans, helping to determine price points, product specifications, and product mix.

The second part of your research includes the denim market and industry trends for jeans. This should include the following areas:

* Sales trends in the jeans market

* Technological trends in the denim market and their impact on jeans

* Leading manufacturers of denim and where are they located

* Market conditions for denim and *labor* costs for production

* Types of finishes, colors, treatments, and fabrication blends for denim

* Newest styles of jeans, and preferred colors, finishes, and blends

* Product requirements (uniqueness, body-conscious fit, price constraints, comfort, status, or celebrity endorsement)

* Most popular labor market for the production of denim jeans

* Most popular details, findings, and trims for jeans for your market

* If available, selling history of other branded jeans within your organization

There are many sources available to you to do your research. A few sources of textile and fiber information can be found at:

* Cotton Incorporated: www.cottoninc.com

* Just-style: www.just-style.com

* *Apparel News:* www.apparelnews.net

* *Bobbin:* www.bobbin.com/bobbin/index.jsp

* Infomat: www.fashionwire.com/Catalogs/denimcollections.html

* Textile Web: www.textileweb.com/content/homepage/default.asp

You will research fashion trend information for your segment of the denim jeans market. Professionals use fashion-forecasting companies such as Promostyl or The Donegar Group. These organizations provide information on color, silhouette, fabrication, and fashion trends for each industry segment. They look forward about 12 to 18 months, and a retailer or manufacturer makes a significant investment to receive this cutting-edge information. Industry publications also provide trend information about specific markets, such as *Women's Wear Daily* (*WWD*) and *Fashion Wire Daily* (*FWD*) or www.fashionwiredaily.com for women's wear, *Baby Shop* or *Children's Business* for children's wear, and *Daily News Record* (*DNR*) for men's wear. Both *Apparel* and *Apparel News* offer trade information about the entire fashion industry. Your CD-ROM has trend forecasts for each of the denim market segments also found under Industry Research.

Buyers and product developers also attend trade shows and shop markets both domestically and internationally to identify the trends in major fashion cities such as New York City, Los Angeles, Paris, London, or Barcelona. Remember that a product developer for men's wear would not necessarily shop the same cities as someone working in the junior market.

Color forecasting is very specialized and is key to developing successful fashion merchandise. A seasonal color palette begins development about 24 to 30 months in advance of the selling season. Color forecasting is influenced by fashion trends but also politics, economics, demographics, and world events. There are very specific forecasting services, such as the Color Association of the United States and The Color Marketing Group, that supply color trends and seasonal palettes for most major manufacturers and retail product developers in the United States. A product development team to establish the color palette that is central to several predictions may use the color direction of several forecasters, such as Huepoint, The Color Box, or Promostyl, as well as the color associations.

Fabrication research is done simultaneously with color forecasting. Buyers would attend fabric shows such as Premiere Vision in Paris, International Fashion Fabric Exhibition in New York City, and other fairs that might specialize in their market, such as Ideabiella in Cernobbio, Italy, which features couture and better fabrics for the men's market. These sources of trend information are supplemented by fabric libraries such as the one at Cotton Incorporated, which specializes in cotton fabrics such as denim. These libraries allow a buyer to view many sources of fabrics of similar content at one location, providing a more efficient use of the buyer/product developer's time.

Perry's simulation Steps One and Two are considered the research and line conceptualization stages of the product development process. As stated previously, product development is a complex and multifaceted process that often requires a team of designers and merchandisers to successfully bring products to market. However, there are organizations that modify this process and have individuals develop private-label merchandise for their retail establishments.

Using a minimum of three sources beyond those included on the CD-ROM, your market and trend report should cover the following topics for your segment of the fashion industry:

PART I

1. Scope and size of your segment (men's, misses, junior, or children's) of the fashion industry

2. Age range

3. Size range

4. Unique characteristics of your segment (i.e., purchaser vs. wearer, disposable income, frequency of shopping)

5. Wholesale and retail price points for jeans for your segment

6. Expectations of this segment with regard to: *quality*, fabrication, fit, craftsmanship of jeans, labeling/branding

SIMULATION:
Go to Part III on the CD-ROM and trade publications and Web sites.

7. Key brands and labels in the jeans category of your segment

8. Lifestyle of this customer within the segment

PART II

1. Sales trends in the jeans market

2. Technological trends in the denim market and their impact on jeans

3. Leading manufacturers of denim and where are they located

4. Market conditions for denim and labor costs for production

5. Types of finishes, colors, treatments, and fabrication blends for denim

6. Newest styles of jeans, and preferred colors, finishes, and blends

7. Product requirements (uniqueness, body-conscious fit, price constraints, comfort, status, or celebrity endorsement)

8. Most popular labor market for the production of denim jeans

9. Most popular details, findings, and trims for jeans for your market

Your report should be in the same format as this outline. Use any of the trade publications and Web sites for your specific industry that have been mentioned previously, and do not forget to review your CD-ROM under Industry Research.

CHAPTER 4

STEP THREE

Theme and Inspiration Boards

IN THIS CHAPTER, YOU WILL LEARN:

* How to synthesize research into a cohesive, professional presentation
* How to create professional theme and/or inspiration boards

Upon completing your industry and trend research, Step Three is to create a professional presentation of what you believe are the key elements that influence the direction of your private-label line of denim jeans. The conceptual design process begins with feelings, mood, and a direction for the upcoming season. There are many ways to present this information to management and fellow product developers and buyers but the most common process begins with the collection of swatches, pictures, and colors that create a theme or inspiration for the new collection. Magazines are an excellent source of graphics but should not be limited to fashion magazines. Travel publications offer style and feeling and can even be an inspiration for color. Photographs taken while researching trends can add to the mood of your presentation. A summer vacation to Venice could offer just the right mood and hue from the colorful buildings on the island of Murano. Fabric swatches can be bought from a local store or collected by dissecting an old garment or even a tablecloth. Thrift and vintage stores can offer a retro look with regard to silhouette or style, to be updated with contemporary details or trim. This collection of visuals is melded together in a collage, one-, two-, or three-dimensional, to create a mood for a new season or line. This is the launching point and opening discussion for the direction of the product. It is an exploration of customer lifestyle and preferences in a visual format. It does not offer specific styles or a collection but early emergence of themes and concepts.

An example of an inspiration or theme board might begin with a retrospective of the 1960s and the emergence of jeans as a key fashion item. A buyer might search

FIGURE 04.01 *An example of proximity*
SOURCE: Courtesy of K.C. Ellis

antique stores for old record album covers, collect examples of art popular during this time, and cut small pieces of fabric with "flower power" and bright colors. By combining these elements, the buyer creates a direction to present to management and fellow buyers to test the fashion direction of the line. The presentation would include theme boards and a description of the theme and how it relates to the consumer. This board would be the basis of the next step, the actual product line and a guide to the number of styles by garment classification, price point assessment, and an initial sales plan of production units.

A collection of magazine pictures, stationery, wrapping papers, textiles, or other craft and found images should represent the theme you have chosen but must also transfer to an actual design. Your theme board is the anchor that offers direction to the product developer/designer and is what keeps them on track. The cohesive, easily understood theme or inspiration board produces clear, well-defined line boards.

When collecting and arranging your images, you must keep in mind four principles of design that are essential to controlling the viewers' eyes and the visual organiza-

 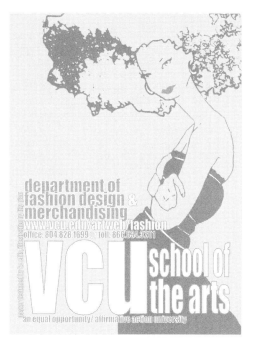

FIGURE 04.02 (LEFT) *An example of right alignment* SOURCE: Courtesy of K.C. Ellis

FIGURE 04.03 (RIGHT) *An example of left alignment* SOURCE: Courtesy of K.C. Ellis

tion. The principles are: proximity, alignment, repetition, and contrast. Begin with proximity, which means to group related items together. This will organize your images and create a cohesive visual presentation. Proximity will provide to the viewer a visual clue expressing your theme (Figure 04.01). The closeness or nearness of the images implies that there is a relationship that you want to convey. Remember that proximity organizes groups of like items to create a visual and intellectual relationship (Williams, pp. 15-21).

Alignment creates a place for every item so that it will foster a visual connection with something else on your board (Figures 04.02 and 04.03). It encourages the viewer to see a relationship between different elements. Proximity organizes related items and alignment attempts to explain the relationship of the groups. Alignment tells the viewer that all the items belong on the presentation board and that the images were not placed indiscriminately but with reason and purpose (Williams, pp. 31-34).

Items can be placed with right, left, or center alignment. All are acceptable but moving items to the right or left of center tends to create more visual interest. Center

FIGURE 04.04 (LEFT) *An example of repetition* SOURCE: Courtesy of K.C. Ellis

FIGURE 04.05 (RIGHT) *An example of contrast* SOURCE: Courtesy of K.C. Ellis

alignment is less sophisticated and can look uninspired. Try moving images around your presentation board to experiment with several different effects. Remember to keep the page unified by aligning every object with the edge of another object. Create visual lines or connections with every element on your board (Williams, p. 81).

The principle of repetition states that you must repeat some element of design throughout your presentation board (Figure 04.04). This emphasizes an element by repeating it so that the viewer knows it is important or trendsetting. Color, shape, and texture are excellent examples of items that when repeated become the glue that keeps your presentation or theme board cohesive. Repetition creates consistency and makes a visual statement.

Finally, contrast adds emphasis by attracting the viewer's eye to two or more dissimilar items (Figure 04.05). Its purpose is to create interest and to add organization to your board. For contrast to be successful and make items jump off a board, the items must be drastically different. Light pink and melon pink just don't create the contrast that hot pink and black create. Be BOLD with your contrast and you will have more effective presentation boards. If you don't create contrast, you will only create conflict. Conflict is not a pleasing element of design or life (Williams, p. 82).

Contrast can be achieved through the use of color, typefaces, spatial relationships, and direction. The use of space or "white space" can also create contrast, as can the boldness of a line. The visual eye finds contrast both pleasing and attractive, and it increases the likelihood of grabbing the attention of the viewer (Williams, p. 85).

Some other helpful hints include creating a focal point. The trend board can seem like a large space with lots of pictures. By creating one item as the center of attention or the focal point, your board will become more interesting and have a stronger presence. You know that you have created a focal point when your eye is drawn to one item immediately upon seeing the board. This focal point can be created through image size but also by using all or any of the principles of design discussed previously.

Remember that when you use text on your board it should be visually strong enough to get the attention of the viewer and allow the message to be understood quickly. The message should make a direct relationship with your theme and be clear, concise, and to the point. Remember that you are not telling a story with words but creating a visual story expressed with images and punctuated with a few words or phrases.

Presentation boards can have many layers. Some are flat and appear almost as a collage. As you become more proficient with design, you can add layers of images to add depth and interest to your inspiration board. This is done by gluing an image to foam core, then carefully cutting it out with a box cutter. If you need to cut a straight line, use your metal ruler as a guide. Use the emery board to finish and smooth the edges, then glue the raised image to the larger board. You will find examples of these types of layered boards as well as examples of the elements of design on the Perry's CD-ROM under the heading Theme and/or Inspiration Board Presentations.

HOW TO PRODUCE A PROFESSIONAL PRESENTATION BOARD

Professional trend boards can make or break a presentation. Computer skills in PhotoShop and Illustrator are helpful but not essential to produce great-looking boards. Begin with a black foam core board cut approximately 20" × 30". Foam core has the body to withstand several presentations and not become ragged or dog-eared, and the black background adds depth and makes color pop. Edges should be taped with either 1 inch of black photography tape or black masking tape. Using a pencil, draw a ¼-inch line around each side of the board as a guide for your tape. Begin with the top and bottom of your board, and then the sides, making sure to extend about

1 inch beyond the actual length of the board. This "tag" or overage allows you to miter or finish the end of your board by trimming and folding the edges underneath and to the back of the board. This first step makes a huge difference in the presentation of the board, as it hides the white foam interior.

Be sure to assemble the tools you will need:

* Rubber cement, white glue, or spray adhesive

* Double-stick tape (permanent kind) or framer's tape

* Scissors, pinking shears, box cutter, and Exacto knife

* A clear ruler 2 inches wide by 18 inches long

* A metal ruler with a cork back

* An emery board or nail file

* Black masking tape ¾ inch wide for edging

* A collection of images that represent your theme (more than what you need)

Here are some additional hints to help you create a professional concept or inspiration board.

* Remember to choose one alignment and stick with it. Do not use a center focal point and then stick images around it. It will look unprofessional and unsophisticated.

* Remember to finish the edges of fabrics by cutting them with pinking shears so that they look finished.

* Make a color copy of fabric and adhere it to your board as done with paper. This way it is not necessary to cut up a favorite or vintage garment.

* Make color copies of favorite images so if you make a mistake you can try over again.

* Remember to smooth the images before the glue dries.

* Use a box cutter on foam core and an Exacto knife on paper images.

* Practice cutting images after you have glued them to the foam core. These will add depth and interest to your board.

* When layering boards, use the emery board or nail file to smooth the edges of anything that isn't cut exactly straight.

* Do not put extraneous items on your board that will either fall off or become tattered after use (i.e. cotton balls for snow or M&M's for Christmas decorations).

* Let each layer dry before adding another layer. Often rubber cement works better than spray adhesive.

* Give yourself about three or four days to complete a presentation board.

* Practice, practice, practice.

Once you have assembled your supplies and images, you are ready to begin assembling your board. Following the directions above, create an inspiration or theme board for your product development concept for denim jeans for your department. Be sure to follow the principles of design and hints stated above.

SIMULATION: *Go to Part IV on the CD-ROM and do your own research.*

CHAPTER 5

STEP FOUR

Design and Concept Boards

IN THIS CHAPTER, YOU WILL LEARN:

* How to synthesize concepts into actual product presentation boards

* How to create professional presentation of your proposed line of jeans

* How to address value from a consumer's perspective and from a manufacturers perspective

Upon completing your inspiration boards, Step Four is to create a professional presentation of what you believe are the key silhouettes and shapes and the actual line drawings or "*flats*" of your private-label line of denim jeans. The conceptual design process begins with feelings, mood, and a direction for the upcoming season that you created in step three with your concept board. Now you will translate those feelings into actual garments. There are many ways to present this information to management and fellow product developers and buyers, but the most common process begins with the collection of swatches, pictures, colors, illustrations, and flats that create the new collection.

At this point in the product development process, the buyer/product developer would work directly with or turn over the creation of the line to a designer. *Prototypes* for the silhouette, including details such as pockets, trims, zippers, and any adornment, would be illustrated in a sketch. The interpretation of the concept board must also consider practical aspects such as the target market and key price points. Sometimes items are purchased from other markets or from vintage stores to act as a catalyst for the new line. For example, the junior buyer at Perry's might purchase a very upscale, designer jean that retails for $250.00 and give this to the designer to interpret into an innovative but salable item at a much lower price point. Every organization uses its own method of line creation, including the use of market research, trend forecasting, shopping the market and competition, purchase of new and/or vintage garments, and

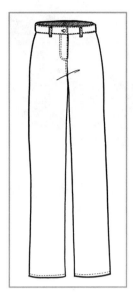

FIGURE 05.01
*Example of junior
flat drawing*
SOURCE: Courtesy of
Noelle McKown

viewing fashion from the streets to the runway as well as magazines and the Internet.

The designer would begin with a number of quick sketches called *croquis* that are an initial interpretation of the concept board and market research. These croquis or working sketches for an entire line might fill a sketchbook, depending on the designer's style, and would be the basis of the new products to be explored and adapted as the line concept is finalized. From the croquis, the designer would refine the sketches and develop a series of flats, or blueprints, to show how the garment would be constructed. These flats can be done by hand but today are often done on the computer through a CAD (Computer-Aided Design) program to illustrate the pattern pieces and details of the garment. Figure 05.01 is an example of a flat sketch for a junior jean. There are also several flat drawings for all categories of jeans on your CD-ROM located within each industry segment in Part III (mens, misses/juniors, or childrens).

The product development team must always keep the consumer in mind when designing the product line. Style, of course, is paramount but unit price and perceived value are equally as important to the design team. Today's consumers not only want to look great but also to feel like they have received great value. This means delivering merchandise that has visual appeal and meets the price point that customers are willing to spend.

According to www.just-style.com, "The Top 8 Shopping Trends" (June 28, 2004), more than 66 percent of women between 18 and 70 years old consider "price" to be the most important element of the purchase decision, ranking this as number one in their trend list. They ranked "value" as number two, noting that 59 percent of the women surveyed asked themselves, "Is this good use of my money?"

The merchandiser or buyer often takes the role of delivering the goods at the right price. This takes compromise within the product development team, changing the many specifications that drive up the cost of a product. Discussions of fabrication, buttons, zippers, stitching, design details such as embroidery and embellishment, *finishing*, packaging, labels, and hangtags are all considerations that the team would tackle to deliver the best product at the best price.

The jeans classification is worn by men, women, and children, but women's and children's pants usually have more details and a wider variation of styles. The silhouette

FIGURE 05.02

Example of design board

SOURCE: Courtesy of Tam Nguyen, Erica Chavis, and Priscilla Lynch

for jeans would vary with the leg width and length. Straight, boot-cut, flared, or wide legs are often part of the design silhouette but fit also comes into play. Slim, regular, or baggy fit helps define the jean silhouette and specifications. Garment details help define the style, including:

* Zipper versus button fly

* Pocket size, style, and placement

* Seams and stitching

* Thread color

* Waistband width and style

* The drop, or where the jean sits relative to the waist

* Adornment

* Buttons or snaps

These are many of the decisions the designer and merchandiser must make based on their target market and price points. Figure 05.02 is an example of a concept board for a denim line. Review your CD-ROM under Design and Concept Board Presentations

TABLE 05.01

DEPARTMENTAL PRICE RANGES

PRICE RANGE	CATEGORY
$25-35	Entry level
40-75	Moderate
80-150	Designer

TABLE 05.02

DEPARTMENTAL PRICE RANGE AND INVENTORY $ TO BE SPENT AT RETAIL

PRICE RANGE	CATEGORY	%	$
$25-35	Entry level	35%	$ 35,000
40-75	Moderate	40	40,000
80-150	Designer	25	25,000
Total Dollar Plan for Jeans (at Retail)			$100,000

for more examples of line development boards illustrating the use of visuals, fabrication, sketches, and flats. These examples are of student work using PhotoShop, Illustrator, Lectra's U4ria CAD system, and a combination of these various techniques.

Planning any assortment requires a sales projection based on last year's sales records in both dollars and units. This projection looks to optimize the sales of any item that has performed exceptionally well in the previous few seasons. The analysis would track sales by style, color, brand, sizes, and price point. The buyer/product developer wants a balanced stock that provides the right merchandise at the right time, in the right amount, at the right price, and without being overstocked. **Profit** and/or gross margin are also key factors in planning a new product line. There must be a dollar incentive to creating a new line of jeans rather than buying an existing brand.

TABLE 05.03

DEPARTMENTAL ASSORTMENT PLAN BY PRICE POINT AND UNITS

PRICE RANGE	AVG $	CATEGORY	%	$	UNITS /PURCHASE
$25-35	$ 30	Entry level	35%	$ 35,000	1167
40-75	55	Moderate	40	40,000	727
80-150	100	Designer	25	25,000	250
Total Dollar Plan for Jeans				$100,000	

A model stock plan is produced by the product development team that identifies how many styles of classification such as jeans will be carried in each department. This plan includes brands, size range, color assortment, and price points. For example, the model stock for jeans may begin with establishing three distinct price ranges such as those listed in Table 05.01.

The buyer would then take the classification plan in dollars and divide up the total dollar amount to be spent on jeans into three price ranges based on an assigned percentage based on last year's sales figures (Table 05.02).

This can then be translated into units by taking an average price within each price range and dividing the dollars by the average price point to get the number of units projected to give the department a balanced stock. There is an example of this step in developing an assortment plan in Table 05.03. The six-month dollar plan, the assortment plan, and the buyer's responsibilities are described in much more detail in *Perry's Department Store: A Buying Simulation for Juniors, Men's Wear, Children's Wear, and Home Fashion/Giftware.*

The buyer/product developer now has a plan for the approximate number of units needed for each price range and can think about the units to be assigned to each brand, including the private-label line that is being developed. This planning strategy controls the number of SKUs (Stock Keeping Units) to maximize efficiency. A retailer can provide too many styles so that the customer becomes confused or the retailer loses its brand identity. Also, it is very difficult to track an assortment that contains so many styles that none becomes significant or makes a performance or fashion statement.

Organizations that produce staple goods may limit the number of styles but expand the line with broader assortments of colors and sizes. This basic assortment that has few styles is considered narrow but deep because it carries many colors and sizes in each style. Specialty chain stores typically carry narrow and deep assortments while better specialty and some department stores will have broad (many styles) and shallow (few colors and sizes) assortments.

SIMULATION:

Go to Part II and Part V on the CD-ROM.

You are now ready to produce your line of denim jeans based on your research and your inspiration board. Using the examples of design and concept boards on your CD-ROM, create a product line presentation board(s) with a minimum of two different styles of jeans and a maximum of four styles for your department. You will produce and import a total of 2,400 pairs of jeans to be distributed to your five stores for the next season. Styles can be developed in different fabrications but each style should be produced in the same size range that is standard for your segment of the jeans market.

Knowing that many students using this text are not fashion designers nor have access to an artist, you can use the flats from the CD-ROM that appear in each Industry Research segment as a basic silhouette and adapt them to your specifications. Print out the flats from your computer, adapt or embellish the sketches, and photocopy your design for your board. There are many examples of student work on the CD-ROM under the heading Design and Concept Board Presentations that will show different methods and variations.

You may also create a *line list* that includes only the flat drawings with fabrication recommendations and a suggested retail price for future reference. Many manufacturers use a line list as a guide or catalog of the different styles to present their current season of clothing. A line list is used by sales representatives or product developers when showing the line because it indicates a line drawing or silhouette, style number, brief description of the garment, price, and approximate delivery date for each garment. This line list can be adapted as you move through the remaining steps of the product development process. For example, the next chapter discusses fabrication, and with that new information you may update your fabrication specifications and change the price points accordingly.

For the sake of time, you are not required to produce an assortment plan but you should be aware of the importance of planning in both dollars and units for your departmental assortment. Your instructor may choose to use the assortment plan that was created in your Perry's buying simulation if you have already studied that part of the buying process.

CHAPTER 6

STEP FIVE

Choosing the Best Fabrications, Findings, and Trims

IN THIS CHAPTER, YOU WILL LEARN:

....

* The importance of choosing the proper fabrics and trims for your jeans program
* Some of the finishing and trim options available, and the impact of the addition of these elements on the cost of the finished product
* The factors involved in choosing the best location for sourcing the fabrics, trims, and labor to produce blue jeans, and the impact of quotas and duty on the delivery of the desired product
* Variables in cost of fabrics and labor from three distinctly different parts of the world, and the importance of cost of materials and production on the decision of where to source the product
* The ramifications to costing of adding design details to your product, such as embroidery, extra trim, and special fabric treatments

....

Your earlier research has prepared you with evaluations of your target customer, target competition, and specific needs of your store's denim jeans department (for either men, women, juniors, or children). You have made important decisions concerning whether the jeans that you have identified for your private-label product development project will be basic, updated fashion, or trendy; and you made a presentation on styling and fabric concepts. It is now time to investigate options for choosing and sourcing the best fabrics and trims for your product. Factors in your decision-making process will involve:

1. Availability and cost of basic fabrics

2. Degree of expertise and ability of local suppliers to perform desired treatments to fabric

3. Access to desired trims, or knowledge of cost to transport these trims from another locale to the production plant

4. Cost to produce and transport finished product from the country of origin to Perry's warehouse in the United States

5. Impact of quotas and duty on the pricing decision

PREPLANNING

Prior to initiating the process of finding fabrics, trims, and sources for manufacturing your garments, make sure that you have done due diligence to determine that you have chosen retail price points that fit into your assortment plan and the merchandise mix of your department. Equally important, you must compare your planned retail price points with those of identified retail competitors to ensure that your target customers will be willing to spend at least part of their jeans budget in your store.

In Chapter 3, your research focused on important aids to assist in making this determination, such as visiting stores in your area that you determined to be competitors to Perry's, consulting fashion magazines and newspapers that cater to your target customer, and searching Internet sites and catalogs of retailers who appeal to the primary consumer.

At this point, it is a good idea to revisit stores that carry jean styles in fabrics that are similar to the ones in which you are interested. Pay attention to the information on labels, such as fiber content, country of origin (where the garment is manufactured), and type of finish on the fabric.

FABRIC SELECTION

Denim is defined as a type of *yarn-dyed* cotton fabric that has a heavy, *Z-twist twill weave*. In traditional denim, the *warp* yarns are dyed *indigo* and the *weft* yarns are left a natural color to achieve the kind of two-tone effect that we have all come to recognize. Typically, denim fabrics are of medium weight at about 10½ to 12 ounces per square yard.

Technology and fashion, however, have opened up many new options to those who design and produce denim jeans. In addition to the standard weight described above, product developers can also choose heavyweight denim of about 13 to 14 ounces. These weights are sometimes selected for garments that will undergo harsh finishing techniques (to be discussed later in the chapter). They also have the option of lightweight denim of approximately 7 to 10 ounces per square yard, whose advantages include a softer *hand* and increased drapability.

In addition to weight variances, one can choose to purchase denim fabrics whose yarns are either ***ring spun***, a more expensive process that results in a smoother, stronger fabric, or ***open-end spun***, an economical choice that delivers coarser fabrics that are not as strong as those of ring-spun yarns. Typically, ring spun is the choice for higher retail price points in department and specialty stores, while open end would be the natural selection for value-priced jeans in chain and discount stores.

While denim for many years was made of 100 percent cotton, there are many other options today for fabric blends that change and enhance the look and performance of basic denim fabrics. Some of these are the following:

* Cotton/***spandex*** blends accommodate a variety of body types and add to the fit and comfort of the jeans

* Cotton/polyester blends can serve a variety of purposes. The polyester may be added to increase strength and soften the hand, to add a sheen to the fabric, or to give it a flatter finish

* Cotton/ramie blends have been used for cost control and quota issues

* Tencel is a new natural fiber (introduced in the 1970s) that offers an interesting addition to denim fabrics. It adds strength, softness, and a more luxurious hand

* Specialty blends such as cotton/wool and cotton/nylon/silk are not usually selected for volume-priced jeans but may appear in some designer or better brands

At the same time that you are researching and deciding upon your fabric blend and weight, it is important to consider the finishes that are available for your selection. The look, hand, and performance of the final product can be greatly affected by the combination of the fabric and the finish choice. It is even possible to produce a jean that has multiple finishes, but it is imperative that you remember that each time a finishing process is added, you must also add to the wholesale cost of the final product.

There are many choices for finishing techniques available to the product developer, but some of the more common ones are described below.

* Garment washing is a final step in production in which the jeans are actually commercially washed for the purpose of fading the color and imparting a softer hand and a worn or vintage look. Often chlorine bleach is added to create the desired effect, but other additive choices are ammonia or potassium.

* *Stonewashing* has evolved from the original procedure in which actual stones were tossed into the washing machine. Today, the effect can be achieved through the addition of *pumice stones*, enzymes, sand, ceramic balls, and other harsh elements.

* Distressing of jeans to make them look old, worn, or vintage is accomplished by subjecting the fabrics or finished garments to a variety of cruel-sounding procedures such as grinding, *hand sanding*, resin applications, baking in an oven, napping, using a hot iron to wrinkle the fabric, and *sandblasting*.

* Overdyeing is another way to change the color of the basic indigo blue denim jean. In this procedure, the yarns that make up the fabric are dyed black, and then the fabric is overdyed again with black to create a deep, saturated tone.

There are some extra finishes that can be added to the jeans to improve performance or to create an effect. Special additives can help to make the jeans stain- and water-resistant or even flame-resistant. The fabric can be mercerized with an alkali treatment to make it stronger and more accepting of dye, to create deep tones. It can be calendered to create a well-pressed product with very saturated color. Again, all of these extra processes greatly add to the cost of manufacturing the jeans.

Additional information on denim finishes, fabrics, and terminology can be found in the glossary, as well as in the *Women's Wear Daily* article "No Uncertain Terms" in Part III of the CD-ROM.

TRIMMING THE JEANS

In addition to the standard trims that can be found on jeans, such as zippers, buttons, *grommets*, and pockets, fashion trends and new innovations in some seasons create the need/desire for extra embellishments. Some of these may be:

* Extra zippers, pockets, stitching details

* Leather trims or even more unusual choices (feathers?)

* Jewels and sequins

* Embroidery

* Patches

* Printing, embossing, or laminating

Each of these will also boost significantly the cost price of the basic jean, and the prices for these extras must be weighed against the expected increase in sales of the garment as a result of the addition of a particular trim.

FABRIC AND LABOR SOURCING

This simulation allows you to select from one of three areas of the world for sourcing your fabrics, trims, and labor: (1) Mexico/Caribbean, (2) China/Far East, or (3) Turkey/ Eastern Europe. Although there are certainly differences between prices and manufacturing conditions in, for example, Mexico versus the Caribbean basin, there are enough similarities to the regions that one can group them for the purposes of a simulation. In another textbook, *Perry's Department Store: An Importing Simulation*, you will have the opportunity to delve further into the issues surrounding the importing of blue jeans.

An important part of the duties of a buyer/product development manager is to evaluate the best sources for fabric, findings, trim, and labor. In some organizations, there are large teams of people whose jobs revolve solely around these activities. In smaller companies with a limited budget and fewer product development team members, this often becomes the job of the buyer or head merchandiser.

Research, prior experience, interviews, and traveling to mills and factories in key parts of the world can each be a part of the process of identifying the right sources for your blue jeans program. It is crucial to consider all of the important factors in the journey of your product from raw materials to your selling floor. In order to guarantee a satisfied customer, the merchandiser must understand and be certain of excellence in the following:

* Raw materials are readily available and of the type that will work best for your garments

* Fabric mills are conveniently located to the sewing factories, or that ease of transportation from mill to factory is assured

* Selected sewing factory has the production capability and the expertise to be able to make your order in a timely manner

* Quality control is built into each step of the production cycle

* Quota is available and duty rates understood and factored into the equation. *Duty* rates will be discussed in Chapter 8 when we complete **cost sheets**.

A word or two about quota: Buyers must be up-to-date on issues involving quotas. Quota restrictions have long been a much debated issue around the world, and the buyer must stay current on the most recent government regulations applicable to the General Agreement on Tariffs and Trade (GATT), the World Trade Organization (WTO), the North American Free Trade Agreement (NAFTA), and the Caribbean Basin Initiative (CBI). As quotas on some categories of merchandise are lifted, the impact on the buyer's ability to import goods can be greatly impacted.

Table 06.01 shows a list of major manufacturing countries of the world with their rankings of denim fabric exports to the United States (year ending Jan. 2004). Table 06.02 gives information about the number of denim jeans and jackets imported in the year 2003 to the United States from the top ten export countries. Table 06.03 lists some advantages to each of the three world areas for sourcing of your fabrics, trimmings, and final jean products. Table 06.04 indicates approximate costs for fabric and labor in the three selected world areas.

Figure 06.01 is an example of a fabric detail sheet. You will find a blank copy of this form in Figure 06.02 and on the CD-ROM.

You are now ready to choose the denim fabric(s), findings, trim, and areas of the world where you will source these components, as well as secure manufacturing space.

YOUR STEP-BY-STEP PLAN

STEP I   Review design or concept boards from your presentation to ensure that you are comfortable with styling, theme, color story, fabric direction.

STEP II   Review target customer profile, competitive situation, and plans for other branded and non-branded denim programs within your own store assortment to assess your needs for this private-label program. Determine retail price points and planned gross margin for the collection.

SIMULATION:
Go to Tables 06.01
through 06.04
in the book and
Figure 06.02
in the book or
CD-ROM.

STEP III   Using Tables 06.01 through 06.04 as a starting point, research and compare prices and pros/cons of sourcing in the three world areas detailed there. Make your selections and justify your choices in writing. Begin to make a list of cost prices for fabric, finishes, findings, and trim. You will use this information for your cost sheet exercise in Chapter 8, Step Seven.

TABLE 06.01

BLUE DENIM FABRIC IMPORTS

COUNTRY	IMPORTS YEAR ENDED JAN. 31	PERCENTAGE CHANGE	SHARE OF U.S. IMPORTS
MEXICO	31.1 million SME	-38.9 percent	32.6 percent
CANADA	17.9 million SME	36.7 percent	18.8 percent
HONG KONG	15.9 million SME	-47.1 percent	16.8 percent
TAIWAN	11.4 million SME	-59.5 percent	12.0 percent
ITALY	5.5 million SME	70.6 percent	5.8 percent
JAPAN	4.0 million SME	75.1 percent	4.2 percent
INDONESIA	1.5 million SME	-80.0 percent	1.5 percent
INDIA	1.5 million SME	-29.7 percent	1.5 percent
TURKEY	1.4 million SME	-64.4 percent	1.5 percent
MALAYSIA	1.1 million SME	-60.9 percent	1.2 percent
WORLD	95.7 million SME	-37.8 percent	100.0 percent

SME = Square Meters Equivalent
SOURCE: Office of Textiles & Apparel, U.S. Department of Commerce. *Women's Wear Daily*, May 27, 2004, Section II, p.14.

TABLE 06.02

U.S. DENIM JEANS AND JACKET IMPORTS

COUNTRY	IMPORTS YEAR ENDED JAN. 31	PERCENTAGE CHANGE	SHARE OF U.S. IMPORTS
MEXICO	17.6 million dozen	-8.8 percent	44.2 percent
HONG KONG	1.6 million dozen	-21.4 percent	4.1 percent
CAMBODIA	1.6 million dozen	30.0 percent	4.0 percent
COSTA RICA	1.5 million dozen	-9.4 percent	3.8 percent
GUATEMALA	1.4 million dozen	6.0 percent	3.6 percent
VIETNAM	1.3 million dozen	75.8 percent	3.1 percent
COLOMBIA	1.1 million dozen	31.9 percent	2.7 percent
NICARAGUA	943,000 dozen	14.4 percent	2.4 percent
LESOTHO	937,000 dozen	19.7 percent	2.4 percent
EGYPT	835,000 dozen	50.2 percent	2.1 percent

SOURCE: Compiled by the AAFA from Tariff and Trade Data from the U.S. Department of Commerce, U.S. Treasury, and U.S. International Trade Commission. *Women's Wear Daily*, May 27, 2004, Section II, p.14.

TABLE 06.03

SOURCING OPTIONS

CONSIDERATION	MEXICO/CARIBBEAN	TURKEY/E. EUROPE	CHINA/FAR EAST
FABRIC	Limited local availability. Trade Laws dictate source and use.	Few regional producers, but good quality cotton locally grown. Tight pricing disciplines result in higher costs.	Prices low due to government subsidies. Quality varies. Local availability of cotton fabrics and mills for finishing.
TRIM	Limited local availability. Importing components can delay production.	Basic trims available locally. Others must be imported from USA or China.	Easy access to components. Quality and duplication of selections must be closely monitored.
LABOR	Labor prices fluctuate due to local wage controls. Higher turnover of workers can impact learned skills.	Skilled workforce, but limited in numbers. Labor prices higher than other 2 choices.	Nearly unlimited workforce. Government support of industry. Low prices. Moderately skilled workers.
TRADE AGREEMENTS	Favorable to trade with the United States.	Good trade relationships with USA. Some countries (e.g. Bulgaria) have no quota limitations.	High demand for exports can result in limits on availability.
TRANSPORTATION	Boats can get to the United States in as few as 3 days.	Boats to the United States take approx. 18 to 24 days.	Most boats take approximately one month and are subject to many delays.

NOTE: These topics will be covered in more detail in a follow-up textbook, *Perry's Department Store: An Importing Simulation.*

TABLE 06.04

FABRIC AND LABOR COST COMPARISON TABLE

COMPONENTS	MEXICO/CARIBBEAN	CHINA/FAR EAST	TURKEY/EASTERN EUROPE
Denim fabric of 100% cotton basic 14 oz. cloth—cost per linear yard	$2.25	$2.00	$2.75
Added price for lighter weight fashion denim (approx. 12 oz)	+.25	+.20	+.30
Labor per piece—men's jean	1.75	1.50	2.00
Labor—women's	1.75	1.50	2.00
Labor—junior's	1.75	1.50	2.00
Labor—children's	1.50	1.25	1.75

STEP IV   Complete a fabric detail sheet like the one in Figure 06.02 for each of the fabrics in your collection. If you have several styles of jeans that will be made of the same fabric, you need only make one fabric detail sheet for all the styles. However, if you will offer more than one fabric in a particular style, you must put each fabric on a separate fabric detail sheet. If you will offer a print, it must be depicted on a separate fabric detail sheet. The same applies to a yarn-dyed pattern such as a stripe.

COMPLETING THE FABRIC DETAIL SHEET

1. Assign a fabric identification number to each new fabric that will be used in the collection. Develop your own system for numbering and be consistent with the selected format for all fabric identification numbers. One way of numbering is to start with the letter *F* followed by a number, such as #F123. Write that number in the first box on the upper left side of the form.

2. Indicate the season for which the fabric will be used (e.g., F06 could be used for Fall 2006).

3. Give the fiber content in percentages: 100 percent cotton or 80 percent cotton/20 percent spandex.

4. Identify the weight of the fabric: 12 ounces/square yard, for example.

5. Write a brief description of the fabric.

6. Fabric width is usually 58"/60" for denim fabrics, but you should indicate the width of the fabric that you intend to use.

7. Show the cost per yard for your chosen fabric. Remember to add in the extra costs for special finishes, printing, etc.

8. In the middle of the form is room to paste in a swatch of the fabric. Just below that, show color standards for the colors in your solid fabric, or the colors that will be found in your print. For standards, it is best to use a color system such as Pantone® or Scotdic®, but you may also use paint chips or other similar means to show the colors that you have selected for each fabric.

9. At the bottom of the form, on the first line, describe any special finish that the fabric will have. For example: sandblasted, bleached, napped, etc.

10. Next give the washing instructions (most customers want their jeans to be machine washable). Check jeans in catalogs and local stores for representative washing instructions or obtain washing instructions from the denim supplier. Consider also the care instructions for any trim on your garments.

11. The last section is for any miscellaneous information that does not have another space on the fabric detail sheet.

Typically, the buyer would also be required to understand the construction of the denim cloth and would include this information on the fabric detail sheet. For example, one commonly used construction is 72 × 42, which is an indication of the number of picks and wales in the fabric. Further details, such as the size of the yarns, would also be required information. For this simulation, we omit that information, but you may add it to the miscellaneous line if you have access to that information.

Fabric ID #: F123	**Season:** F06
Fiber Content: 100% cotton	**Fabric Weight:** 12 oz/square yard
Description: Gray cast indigo crosshatch broken twill denim	
Fabric Width: 58/60"	**Cost:** $2.50 per yard

Swatch

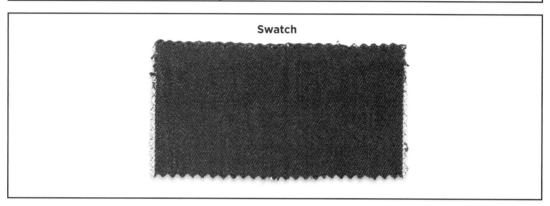

COLOR STANDARDS

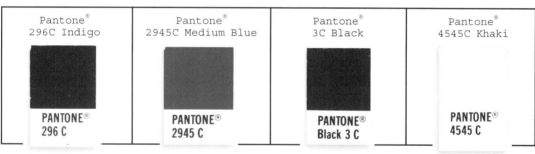

Pantone® 296C Indigo	Pantone® 2945C Medium Blue	Pantone® 3C Black	Pantone® 4545C Khaki
PANTONE® 296 C	PANTONE® 2945 C	PANTONE® Black 3 C	PANTONE® 4545 C

Finish: Enzyme washed
Washing Instructions: Machine wash warm, tumble dry low
Miscellaneous: 72 × 42 construction

FIGURE 06.01   Sample Perry's fabric detail sheet

Fabric ID #:	Season:
Fiber Content:	Fabric Weight:
Description:	
Fabric Width:	Cost:

Swatch

COLOR STANDARDS

Finish:
Washing Instructions:
Miscellaneous:

FIGURE 06.02   *Perry's fabric detail sheet*

CHAPTER 7

STEP SIX

Developing Style Specification Sheets

IN THIS CHAPTER, YOU WILL LEARN:

* How to prepare a preliminary or designer's specification sheet
* The importance of precise and clear communication in order to ensure that the final garments meet all store and customer requirements
* Which steps to follow so that the specification sheet results in the prototype garments that the product development team envisioned

For this simulation, you will prepare the ***specification package*** (or spec pack, as it is commonly called in the industry) in two different stages: (1) in this chapter's work, you will prepare a preliminary or designer's specification sheet, and (2) in Chapter 8, you will learn how to complete a technical specification sheet to include additional parts such as garment size specifications. In the garment industry, there is typically a third set of specification sheets that are prepared by the engineering or production department that would outline in detail how the garment is to be sewn, including cutting instructions and how to put pattern pieces together in the most efficient manner. Because Perry's will use foreign contractors to sew their private-label garments, the contractor's engineers or production department will complete this step.

UNDERSTANDING THE PRELIMINARY SPECIFICATION SHEET

One cannot overemphasize the importance of clear, concise instructions and communication in the preparation and explanation of the details in a specification sheet. Even if the person who is reading the instructions sits in the next office and works for the same company, there is room for misinterpretation and misunderstanding when looking at sketches and information prepared by someone else. Imagine how much more complicated this process becomes when the people reading the specification sheets live and work in another country and probably have a different first language than the person who prepared them. It is crucial that terminologies used be consistent, follow industry standards, and leave no room for confusion. Do not assume that the people reading your document know everything about the proposed garments that you know. When in doubt about how much to explain, overexplain.

The remainder of this chapter will be devoted to a step-by-step simulation of completing a preliminary specification sheet. Use the example in Figure 07.01 as a guide. You will find a blank copy of this form in Figure 07.02 and on the CD-ROM.

DEVELOPING THE PRELIMINARY SPECIFICATION SHEET

Prepare one preliminary specification sheet for each different style in your collection. Use the blank form in Figure 07.02 in the book or the CD-ROM for the simulation.

SIMULATION:

Go to Figure 07.02 in the book or CD-ROM and to your fabric detail sheets.

1. The fabric detail sheets that you completed in Step Five will become the starting point for preparing your preliminary specification sheets. Use the fabric identification number from these sheets on each style specification sheet to which it applies.

2. Prepare a separate specification sheet for each style in your program.

3. If you have not already done so, assign a ***style number*** to each different garment in your jeans assortment. Using the sample guide here and the blank form in the book or on the CD-ROM, enter the style number in the assigned box on the form. It sounds simplistic, but it is important to always use the same style number that you assign here when referring to that garment on all future correspondence.

4. Enter a brief description of the garment on the line provided.

5. Enter the selling season for which the intended style is planned (for example, Fall 2006 is depicted as F06). It is important to note here that, in a category such as jeans, classic styles are often repeated from season to season. If no changes are made to the garment, then the style number would remain the same and only the season would change. If the style has changed (another pocket added, for example), then a new style number should be assigned, and the previous style number should be listed in the appropriate box (here called previous style #) to indicate that the fit and body type are the same.

Style #: 9203   **Previous Style #:** 9103

Season: F06   **Date:** 2/01/06

Description: Misses Boot-cut 6 pocket jean

Fabric #: F123

Type/Fiber content: 100% cotton broken-twill denim

Finish: Enzyme washed

Sketch - Front

Colors/Print/YD Patterns	Percentages of each
Indigo	25%
Medium blue	25%
Black	20%
Khaki	20%
Yarn-dyed black/khaki stripe	10%

FINDINGS/TRIM

	Type/Number	Color	Size	Amount
Snaps/Buttons	Logo shank	Nickel	24L	1
Zipper	YKK#560	Match	4"	1
Thread	G#924 Topstitch	Gold		
Rivets	R377	Nickel		10

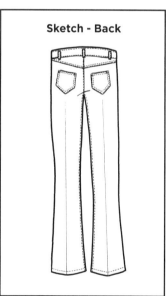

Sketch - Back

Size	6	8	10	12	14	16
Size Scale	1	2	3	3	2	1

DUE DATES

In DC Date: 7/01/06   **Lab dips/Strike-offs:** 2/20/06

Ex Factory Date: 6/01/06   **Prototype sample:** 2/15/06

Cost Price: 2/15/06

FIGURE 07.01   *Sample Perry's style specification sheet*

Style #:   **Previous Style #:**

Season: **Date:**

Description:

Fabric #:

Type/Fiber content:

Finish:

Colors/Print/YD Patterns	Percentages of each

Sketch - Front

FINDINGS/TRIM

	Type/Number	Color	Size	Amount

Sketch - Back

Size						
Size Scale						

DUE DATES

In DC Date: **Lab dips/Strike-offs:**

Ex Factory Date: **Prototype sample:**

Cost Price:

FIGURE 07.02   *Perry's style specification sheet*

6. Enter a brief fabric description, as well as fabric finishing details, in the appropriate boxes. Although you have cross-referenced the number from the appropriate fabric detail sheet, a brief description here will serve to reemphasize the fabric selection for this style—and also hopefully send up a red flag to prompt questions if there are discrepancies between the two documents.

7. Following the fabric information section are a group of boxes that deal with color and print selections. If you plan to offer only solid colors in your denim assortment, then you should list only solid colors in these boxes. If prints are to be included, then assign each a print number (e.g. #P123). If the print comes in more than one color way, then add an indicator to the end of the print number to identify the primary color in the print (e.g. #P123W might refer to a white floral print on a blue denim ground, whereas #P123R could be used to designate a red paisley print on a white denim ground). It is important to note at this point that should you decide to offer prints in your collection, you will need to attach a separate sheet with a copy of the print as described in Chapter 6. The same holds for yarn-dyed patterns such as woven-in stripes. This section should be completed with a breakdown of the percentages of each color, print, print color way, and/or yarn-dyed pattern that will make up the assortment for this particular style.

8. The next section of the specification sheet is for the details on findings and trim that should appear on your garment. Fill in specifics on components such as buttons, zippers, elastic, stretch rib, buckles, grommets, decorative stitching, embroidery, add-ons (glitter, jewels, patches, etc.), or thread (note any special requests here, such as color of thread or if you require an unusual type of thread such as heavier embroidery thread for *topstitching*). Buyers would have access to the lines of trim and findings suppliers for selection, but you may find assistance in the identification of these components by shopping a fabric store or craft shop. Purchase any components that might not be common usage and attach those to the specification sheets. For example, it is not necessary to attach a zipper if it is a common one used for jeans—just specify length, color, and whether it should be metal or plastic. You would, however, want to attach a sample of a particular patch or add-on, such as a jewel or special braid trim. Should you select a button or type of closure that is different from common usage, include that also.

9. If your garment is to have embroidery, you will need to show the design. For the simulation, you can either draw a design or use one that you find on another garment (color copy) or in a catalog or magazine. Assign the embroi-

dery a number (such as E12) and put that number and a depiction of the embroidery on a separate sheet to be included with your specification package. Include that same embroidery number with a brief description of the embroidery on your specification sheet.

10. The same system applies to any screen print or placement print, such as the face of a rock star (in the real world, you *would* need the star's permission) that you intend to put on your garment. Use a separate sheet to depict the image, assign it a number, and refer to it on the appropriate line on the specification sheet.

11. Your specification sheet should include a sketch of both the front and back of your garment. This sketch should show details and give specific information such as size and placement of pockets, size and number of belt loops (e.g. 1¾" × ⅜"), width of waistband, and placement of any topstitching. If your jean has any particular styling features that might affect cost (such as an extra-wide leg), you should indicate that at this time.

12. You will need to show a size range and size scale at this time. Refer back to your target customer research and decide, if you have not previously done so, what sizes will be offered in each jean style. Then decide what the size breakdown will be for each. This is normally done in a prepack of either 6 or 12 pieces. The distribution of your size scale will depend upon your customer profile and what you have learned about the sizes of customers in your selling area. To assist you in this decision, check catalogs or Internet sites or visit stores in your area to see which sizes they offer and try to determine (in stores) how many pieces the buyer bought per size.

13. The last section on the specification sheet deals with due dates. It is here that your production calendar becomes very useful. You have already decided on a season for selling the jeans in Perry's and from that, a delivery date for the goods to be shipped to each of Perry's stores. To accomplish this, a date needs to be established for the jeans to arrive in Perry's distribution center (referred to as DC on the specification sheet) that will allow time for processing, paperwork, packing, and shipping to each store. This time frame differs by season and by store needs, but figure three weeks' time to be safe. Put that "In DC" date on the specification sheet. Based on the average (or maybe worst-case scenario) time that it takes for garments to ship from your selected country of origin and arrive at your distribution center, enter an expected "Ex factory date" on the specifica-

tion sheet. Don't cut the time allowance too close; sometimes lead times become an issue of negotiation when dealing with contract factories.

14. It is also important to enter dates when **lab dips**, **strike-offs**, and prototype samples will be due. This will be clarified in the next section.

15. You will also want to establish a deadline for the preliminary cost from the contracted factory. Depending upon the store's relationship with the contractor and the agreements made, this can either be in the form of a **full package (FP)** price or a **cut, make, and trim (CMT)** price. Full package pricing occurs when the manufacturer (in this case, overseas contractor) provides fabrics, trims, supplies, and labor and quotes one price for a completed garment. Cut, make, and trim refers to a program when the store (or apparel wholesaler) provides designs, fabrics, and trims and the contractor provides only labor and supplies. Consequently, he or she would only quote a price that includes these two elements. For this simulation, we will assume a CMT arrangement. Because most apparel programs are put together under tight time constraints, you should only allow about two weeks for the contractor to quote a CMT price.

16. In the space next to the season, a date should be entered that represents the time when the specification package is sent to the contractor.

LAB DIPS AND STRIKE-OFFS

As discussed in Chapter 6, the fabric detail sheets, as well as any separate sheets for prints and yarn-dyed patterns, will include standards with exact colors that should be duplicated in the correct fabric for buyer approval. When the contractor receives the specification package, he or she will send the color standards to the fabric mill. Strict guidelines must be established to ensure that the colors in your solids, prints, and yarn-dyed patterns are as close as possible to the standards established. It is important to note that colors seen on paper look different in fabric and that different fibers, yarns, and fabrics absorb color differently. The experienced designer or buyer/merchandiser will acquire an "eye" for color and will be able to tell when the fabric is as close to the standard as possible. There are also a number of lighting systems that can be purchased to duplicate store light or daylight and to help standardize color shading and matching.

Solid color approvals will come back from the mill in the form of lab dips, which are pieces (usually 3" × 3" or smaller) of the actual fabric that have been dipped in a mixture of the proposed dye combinations to achieve the standard color. Print strike-offs are one repeat size of the pattern that is to be printed showing actual color placement. We will deal more with these in the next chapter, but allow about two weeks for the mill to prepare these and send them back for approval. Indicate this due date on the specification sheet.

PROTOTYPE SAMPLES

When the contractor receives the specification sheet, he or she will make a first sample or prototype of each different garment in the program. In order to make these garments properly, he or she will need a copy of Perry's size specifications. We will prepare these in the next chapter. Due dates for prototype samples to be completed will vary with the capabilities of the contractor and the number of different prototype samples to be made for each program, but assume a due date of three weeks from the date that the contractor receives all information.

CHAPTER 8

STEP SEVEN

Developing Cost Sheets and Size Specs

IN THIS CHAPTER, YOU WILL LEARN:

....

*   What is needed to complete the balance of the spec pack, including size specification measurements
*   How to develop a preliminary cost sheet
*   The importance of accuracy in production patterns, grading, and **_marker_** making

....

COMPLETING THE SPEC PACK

Now that you have prepared the fabric detail sheets and the preliminary specification sheets (called style specification sheets), it is time to complete the balance of the forms that will make up the total spec pack. When these are finished, you will be ready to send everything off to the contractor and to request: prototype samples, lab dips and/or strike-offs, and final labor prices for each of the styles in your program. In the last chapter, we established due dates for all of these requests and indicated those on the style specification sheets.

There are actually two simulation exercises in this chapter: (1) the first will be to complete the detail and size specification sheets for each style, including key measurements, and (2) the second will be to prepare a preliminary cost sheet for each style.

DETAIL AND SIZE SPECIFICATION SHEETS

Using the blank form in Figure 08.02 in the book or CD-ROM and the sample form in Figure 08.01, complete a detail and size specification sheet for each different jean style in your collection.

SIMULATION:

Go to Figure 08.02 in the book or CD-ROM.

DETAIL AND SIZE SPECIFICATION SHEET

PERRY'S

Style #: 9203 Misses Low Waist Jean | **Season:** FO6

Fabric Content: 100% Cotton broken twill denim

Sketch

Labels	Type/Ref #	Qty	Placement Details
Main Label	PBML Perry's Best Woven	1	Center back waist inside. Flat-edge caught in seam
Care Label	Printed - MWWTD low	1	Wearing left inside SS 10" down from waist
Size Label			Include size on care label

Country of Origin: China

Notes:

Code	Specification	Size 10	Revised
A	Waist (relaxed)TM	32	
B	Low Hip (3" from crotch)TM	38	
C	Front Rise (incl. waistband)	8 $^3/_4$	
D	Back Rise (incl. waistband)	14 $^1/_4$	
E	Thigh (1" down from crotch)TM	22 $^1/_2$	
EE1	Knee (14 $^1/_2$" below crotch)TM	16	
EE2	Bottom Opening TM	19	
F	Inseam	34	
FF1	Outseam (excl. waistband)	40	

Code	Specification	Size 10	Revised
AA1	Belt Loop (L x W)	1 $^3/_4$ x $^3/_8$	
AA2	Waistband Depth	1 $^1/_2$	
AA3	Fly Front (L x W, excl. waistband)	4 x 1 $^1/_4$	
G	Front Pocket from Waist	3	
GG1	Front Pocket from SS	4	
GG2	Watch Pocket (L x W)	4 $^1/_2$ x 4$^1/_4$	
GG3	Back Pocket (L x W)	5 $^1/_2$ x 5	
GG4	Back Pocket from Waist (incl. waistband)	2 $^7/_8$	
GG5	Back Pocket from CB	1 $^3/_8$	

FIGURE 08.01 *Sample Perry's detail and size specification sheet*

PERRY'S

DETAIL AND SIZE SPECIFICATION SHEET

Style #:

Season:

Fabric Content:

Labels	Type/Ref #	Qty	Placement Details
Main Label			
Care Label			
Size Label			

Country of Origin:

Notes:

Sketch

Code	Specification	Size	Revised

Code	Specification	Size	Revised

FIGURE 08.02   *Perry's detail and size specification sheet*

TABLE 08.01

SAMPLE SIZES USED FOR PRODUCT DEVELOPMENT

PRODUCT CATEGORY	APPROPRIATE SAMPLE SIZE
Newborn	6 months or $3/6$
Infant	18 months
Toddler	3T
Girls	5 or XS, and 10 or L
Boys	5 or XS, and 12 or L
Misses	8, 10, or medium
Women's	18W or 20W
Men's tops	40 or medium
Men's bottoms	34W × 32 L

SOURCE: Sandra J. Keiser and Myrna B. Garner (2003). *Beyond Design: The Synergy of Apparel Product Development*, 265. Courtesy of Fairchild Publications, Inc.

To help you with this exercise, consult the list of most common sample sizes in Table 08.01. Find jean styles that are as close as possible to each of the different jeans that you have adopted for your collection. You may use jeans from your own wardrobe or those borrowed from friends, but your measurements will be most accurate if you start with new jeans. Jeans do usually shrink and change shape slightly after repeated washing and wearing. One way to approach this task is to speak to a retail store in your area that carries jean styles that are similar in fit to the ones that you need to measure. Ask to borrow garments for the purpose of measuring for your project. Although measuring sample sizes will give you the information that you will need to complete your size specifications, it is recommended that you measure two additional sizes in order to get a feel for the **grade** of key measurements for each style, or the number of inches between sizes. You may have to fill out some paperwork for the store, and you must be very careful to return the jeans quickly to the store in their original condition with all the tags still on the garments.

While you are shopping for jean styles that are similar to those in your collection, take note of jeans of varied styles in different stores and glean the following information that will be useful in completing the detail and size specification sheets and also the cost sheet, which we will learn about in the next part of this chapter.

* Note country of origin

* Compare types of brand labels and **_care labels_** for method of application, fabric from which they are made, types of brand names used, and wording of care instructions

* Find jeans of the fabrics and finishes that you intend to use and check to see the care instructions that the manufacturers recommend

Now we are ready to complete the form in Figure 08.02, detail and size specification sheet. Again, you will need one of these forms for each of the styles in your collection. These instructions should be followed in order to successfully accomplish this task:

1. Prepare one of these forms for each of the style specification sheets that you completed for the exercises in Chapter 7. These two forms will be sent together.

2. At the top of the form in the spaces provided, enter the same style number that you used previously for the style specification sheet. Next to that, enter the season indicator (such as F06 to denote Fall 2006).

3. In the next space, repeat the fabric that you intend to use for this item. Repeating the information reinforces it for everyone who will work with this item and reduces the possibility of mistakes.

4. In the boxes provided, insert sketches of the front and back of your jeans, showing as much detail as possible.

5. On the style specification sheets, you indicated which trims were to be used. In the next section on this form, you will detail information about labels and where they are to be placed. Before completing this section, you will need to decide what main label (or brand label) you will use. Options for the name on the label are: (a) use the Perry's name only, or (b) devise an original name for this jean style or program that you want to use on the main label. The buyer would, of course, need to protect the store from liability by investigating to be sure that the name is not already owned by another company. If it is a name that the store will probably use again, they would likely want to obtain a copyright for its exclusive use, but you will not need to concern yourself with these

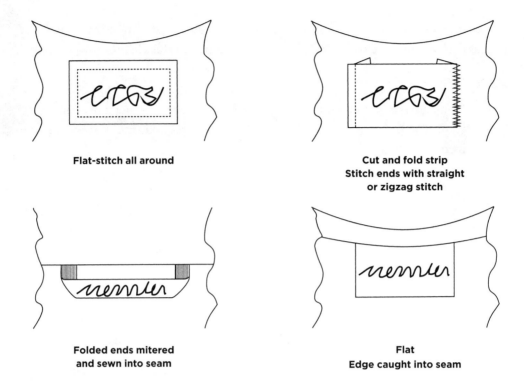

Flat-stitch all around

**Cut and fold strip
Stitch ends with straight
or zigzag stitch**

**Folded ends mitered
and sewn into seam**

**Flat
Edge caught into seam**

FIGURE 08.03

Label attachment methods

SOURCE: Sandra J. Keiser and Myrna B. Garner (2003). *Beyond Design: The Synergy of Apparel Product Development*, 292. Courtesy of Fairchild Publications, Inc.

steps for the simulation. All labels can be either printed or have the name and other writing woven into the label. Typically, printed labels are chosen for budget items or where minimizing cost is particularly critical. You may select either type, but brand labels are most often woven. Figure 08.03 shows examples of the most frequently used types of brand labels. Indicate your selection on the line provided.

6. Next on the form is a section for the type of care label, the location in the garment for the placement of the care label, and the information to be included on the label. Care labels can also be either printed on paper or made with the information woven into the label. The exact wording of the information to be included on care labels is controlled by the Federal Trade Commission (FTC), and the standards are published by the American Society for Testing and Materials (ASTM). Typically, apparel companies have production personnel whose jobs include complete familiarization with these standards. For the purposes of this simulation, you need only state on the detail and size specification sheet the type of care label to be used and cleaning instructions (example: machine wash warm, tumble dry, which would be abbreviated as MWWTD).

7. Next to the line marked Size Label, give instructions for the location of the garment size. You may choose to require a separate size label, or you may just state that the size indicator should appear on the care label.

8. The next line calls for country of origin. Here you should indicate the location where your garments will be produced.

9. The section marked Notes gives you a space to elaborate further on any information that is not completely covered in the other sections of this form.

At the bottom of the form is the place where measurements for the garment should be listed. The sample size is the basis upon which all measurements are determined, and then *grade rules* are applied to calculate the measurements for the remainder of the sizes. Table 08.01 lists the most common sample sizes for the size categories from which you can choose for the simulation.

Some Useful Industry Information
After the sample size has been determined, a pattern-maker will make a master pattern with pattern *blocks* for that size. The other sizes would then be graded up or down by a predetermined scale. This process is still done by hand in some companies, but more often it is accomplished with a computer *grading* system that ensures not only accuracy but a better usage of materials and thus a savings on the cost of the garments. You will not be able to complete this part in your simulation, but you need to understand the entire process.

Back to the Simulation
When measuring a sample (or ideal garment) to establish specification standards, it is important to follow these steps:

* Make certain that the garment to be measured is smooth and wrinkle free. If it is not, iron it.

* Close all zippers, buttons, and fasteners and lay the garment flat on a large table or work space. Smooth it out, but be careful not to stretch it. Jeans are difficult to measure, particularly because the crotch/rise area will not lie completely flat; let the garment lie as naturally as possible. Line up the waistband at center-front and center-back top edges unless you have a jean with a dipped waist or other unusual design feature; in that case, let it lie as it would on the body.

* Lay your tape measure flat on the garment and measure as directed on each line of the specification sheet. Because accurate measurements are difficult to get, measure at least twice for each designated point.

* Some companies record measurements for the waist, seat, etc., in total circumference of the garment; others use flat or half measurements. It is important to note when total circumference measurements are used; this is usually designated by TM (total measurement). For this simulation, we will use TM measurements where applicable.

* Note your measurement in the space provided for the sample size that you have selected. DO NOT round off your measurements. Mark them in ¼- or ½-inch increments. Some measurements (such as collar stands, belt loops on blue jeans, and other small measurements) are even recorded in ⅛-inch increments.

* Consistency of measurement is vitally important and, as with all other information in your spec pack, you need to communicate carefully the way in which you have measured each of your garments.

Let us now take and record measurements for the woman's jean that we have used as an example on the style specification sheet in Chapter 7 and the detail and size specification sheet that we are now preparing.

Note that the first column on the sample form is for a code. This is a designator for each of the required fields on the size specification chart. Some companies use letters to identify measurements needed, others use numbers, and still others use a combination of both letters and numbers. Perry's fit experts would already have a book of codes to be used for all garment measurements, and we will assume for this simulation that they use a combination of letters and numbers. Measure and record in the following manner:

1. Code A: Waist Width (relaxed). This designation is used for woven pants without an elastic waist. If the garment had an elastic waist, it would need to be measured both in a relaxed state and also in a stretched one. Take this measurement from the side of the bottom band to the other side of the bottom band, pulling your tape measure straight across the center of the band. Double this measurement and record in the appropriate box on the form.

2. Code B: Low Hip (3" from crotch). This measurement is also sometimes called Seat Width and sometimes directions are to measure from the waist down. For this garment, start your tape measure from the side seam at a point 3 inches up from the crotch and pull it across the flat garment to the same point on the other side seam. Double the measurement and record it in the designated box on the form.

3. Code C: Front Rise (including waistband). Measure from the top of the waistband on the front of the garment, over the zipper or button placket, following the curve of the front seam, and end at the point where the crotch seams join. Record this as a single measurement.

4. Code D: Back Rise (including waistband). Measure from the top of the waistband on the back of the garment, over the back seam, following the curve of the garment, and end at the point where the crotch seams join. Record this as a single measurement.

5. Code E: Thigh (1" down crotch). Measure just one leg lying flat from the edge/side seam at a point 1 inch down from the crotch straight across the leg, following the leg opening to a point on the opposite edge/side seam. Double this measurement and record.

6. Code EE1: Knee (14½" below crotch). Use same procedure as for thigh, except measure from a point 14½ inches below the crotch on the inside edge/seam and follow the leg opening straight across to the complementary point on the opposite edge/seam. Double the measurement and record.

7. Code EE2: Bottom opening. Measure from the pant leg edge/seam to the opposite pant leg edge/seam on one leg. Measure straight across unless the opening is contoured, in which case you would allow your tape measure to follow the contour, double the measurement, and mark your sheet accordingly.

8. Code F: *Inseam*. Measure from the crotch seam on one leg to the bottom of the leg opening, following the inside leg seam. Record as a single measurement.

9. Code FF1: *Outseam* (excluding waistband). Measure from the bottom of the waistband on one leg to the bottom of the leg opening along the side seam or fold of the garment. Record as a single measurement.

10. Code AA1: Belt Loop (length × width—designated as L×W). Measure the length of one belt loop and then the total length of that loop and record as a single measurement in fractions of ⅛ inch.

11. Code AA2: Waistband Depth (sometimes also called Waist Height). Measure from the waistband upper edge down to the spot where the waistband joins the seam or to the end of the waistband if it is sewn on top. Record as a single measurement.

12. Code AA3: Fly Front (L × W or length × width, excluding waistband). Measure the length from the top of the zipper/fly opening straight down to the bottom of the zipper/fly opening where the **bar tack** might be. Measure the width at the top of the zipper/fly straight across from the fold or edge line to the stitching line on the opposite side of the fly. Record these as single measurements in the format described on the example.

13. Code G: Front Pocket from Waist. Measure one pocket on the front from the waistband top straight down to the top edge of the pocket. Record as a single measurement.

14. Code GG1: Front pocket from SS (side seam): Measure from the side seam straight across to the top of the pocket. Record as a single measurement.

15. Code GG2: Watch pocket L × W (length × width). Measure and record as noted.

16. Code GG3: Back Pocket (L × W). Measure the length to the lowest point and width of one back pocket and record as noted.

17. Code GG4: Back Pocket from Waist (including waistband). Measure from the top of the waistband straight down to the top edge of one pocket. Record as a single measurement.

18. Code GG5: Back Pocket from CB (center back). Measure distance from center back seam straight across to nearest top edge of one pocket and record as single measurement.

19. If any of your jeans have styling features in addition to those listed in this example, then you should list those singularly, following these measurements. For example, your jeans might have cuffs and you would need to measure the height of the cuff and note that. You might have pleats and you would need to indicate their placement on the garment. For more complete information about size specifications, there are a number of good technical manuals available, such as the *Complete Guide to Size Specification and Technical Design* by Paula J. Myers-McDevitt.

PREPARING PRELIMINARY COST SHEETS

The final document that you will need to prepare before sending your completed spec pack to the contractor is the preliminary cost sheet. As with the other forms in your pack, you will need to prepare a separate cost sheet for each of the different styles in your collection. There are several reasons for preparing a cost sheet at this stage, but the main one is to get a fairly accurate reading of what the retail cost of each jean in your collection will be, based upon application of your required *markup* to the total of all costs involved in the manufacture of each style. It is quite common in today's competitive marketplace for the product developer to make adjustments after calculating the preliminary cost sheet. If it seems that the retails calculated will be too high to allow your assortment to be competitively attractive to your target customer, you may want to make some adjustments. Examples of these possible adjustments are: Find less expensive fabrics, minimize the number and type of finishes that you intended to apply to your fabrics or garments, plan for fewer or less expensive trims, and look for ways to lower shipping and handling expenses. A more common adjustment in today's marketplace is to attempt to negotiate a lower labor price with the contractor. Sometimes this can be done if the number of units in your order will be large enough to make it possible for him or her to operate more efficiently (economies of scale).

SIMULATION:

Go to Figure 08.05 in the book or CD-ROM.

* First assemble all the forms that you have previously prepared for your spec pack for each of your styles.

* Research the yardage that you will need for each of the components in each of your styles.

* Determine costs for your fabrics and trims by consulting the fabric cost chart in Chapter 6, searching for fabric and trim suppliers on the Internet from your chosen country of origin, interviewing buyers and apparel wholesalers, and shopping fabric and trim stores to estimate wholesale cost based on retail store prices. Although a buyer/product developer would have wholesale representatives from fabric and trim companies from various countries at her or his disposal and would attend fabric and trim trade shows for cost and availability of components, you may have to do some deep research to get this information. A field trip to a fabric and trim trade show is an excellent source of information.

* Using the blank form in Figure 08.05 in the book or CD-ROM and the sample in Figure 08.04, prepare cost sheets for each of the garments in your collection.

The first step in preparing your preliminary cost sheet is to take an accurate yardage for the fabrics and trims that you will use in each of your styles of jeans.

Measuring Accurate Yardage

This process is most often done by a production engineer or pattern-maker who is skilled and knowledgeable of the ways to lay out pattern pieces in order to get the most economical yield to the fabric. This step is particularly crucial to the realization of an acceptable ***profit margin*** for each of the styles in the collection. Some apparel manufacturers still do this process manually, but most have adopted computerized systems that are easier to manipulate than the manual process, save considerable time, and produce extremely accurate results. Even if the computer marking and grading system saves ½ yard per dozen garments, it is easy to see that this could amount to a sizable savings when multiplied over thousands, or even tens of thousands, of garments.

Final ***fabric consumption***, or the amount of fabric that will be needed to produce the total number of pieces that you will order of each style, will be impacted by such factors as: (1) the number of sizes offered and the size scale, or the number of pieces per size in each pack of your order, and (2) the measurements for each of the sizes offered. Here again, computerized marking and grading prove to be considerable time and money savers.

Style #: 9203   **Date:** 2/01/06

Description: Boot Cut 6 pocket jean   **Season:** F06

Fabric: 12 oz. Gray cast indigo crosshatch broken twill denim

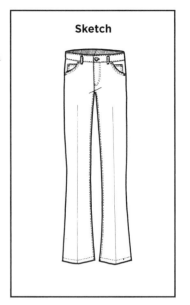

Sketch

Size	6	8	10	12	14	16
Size Scale	1	2	3	3	2	1

Material	Yardage	Price	Cost
Denim 58" wide	1.5	2.20	$3.30
Total Material			$3.30

Trim/Findings	Quantity	Price	Cost
Zipper 4"	1	.25	$.25
Logo Button 24L	1	.05	.05
Thread	1	.15	.15
Rivets	10	.03	.30
Main Label	1	.05	.05
Care Label	1	.02	.02
Hang tag/price tkt	1	.04	.04
Packaging	1	.15	.15
Total Trim			$1.01

Labor	Cost
Cutting/Sewing	$1.50
Enzyme Wash	$1.00
Total Labor	$2.50

	Description	Cost
Shipping	$8.00 per dozen	$.67
Duty	16.6% of labor/material	$1.13
Overhead	18% of cost	$1.23

Total Manufacturing Cost: $9.84

Markup: 60.6%

Retail Price: $25.00

FIGURE 08.04   *Sample Perry's cost sheet*

Style #:   **Date:**

Description: **Season:**

Fabric:

Size						
Size Scale						

Material	Yardage	Price	Cost
Total Material			

Trim/Findings	Quantity	Price	Cost
Total Trim			

Labor	Cost
Total Labor	

	Description	Cost
Shipping		
Duty		
Overhead		

Total Manufacturing Cost:

Markup:

Retail Price:

Sketch

FIGURE 08.05 *Perry's cost sheet*

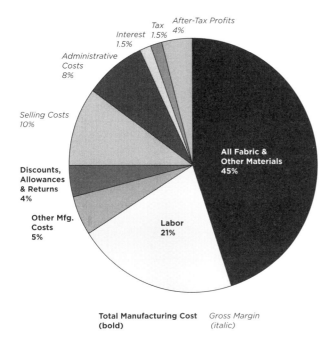

FIGURE 08.06

Cost distribution for a cotton jean

SOURCE: ©1997 American Apparel & Footwear Association

Once the initial measurements for the sample size are determined, the computer will calculate the measurements for all other sizes by using preestablished grade rules for the desired number of inches between each size.

Back to the Simulation

If you do not have access to production engineering students or student pattern-makers who can assist in calculating yardages for this project, you can make estimates by visiting a fabric store. Consult pattern books and find jean bodies (or pant bodies) that are similar in shape to the ones in your collection. Look at the size that matches your sample size and see what yardages they recommend for fabrics and trims. You will want to make sure that you are using the yardages that correspond to the width of the fabrics that you intend to use. You may have to consult several pattern books and several styles in order to "build" the bodies in your collection.

Some apparel companies prepare cost sheets based on one dozen garments, but we will prepare our cost sheets for one garment.

Figure 08.06 is a chart that illustrates a typical breakdown of costs incurred in manufacturing a cotton jean. Since our cost sheets will be calculated for Perry's retail stores, we will add in the markup and additional costs incurred by a retail store.

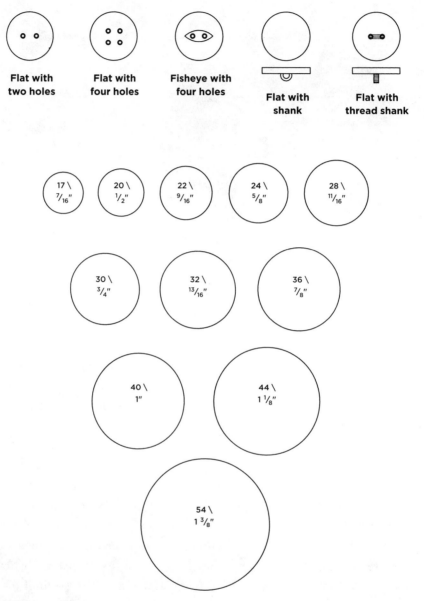

FIGURE 08.07

Types and sizes of buttons

SOURCE: Sandra J. Keiser and Myrna B. Garner (2003). *Beyond Design: The Synergy of Apparel Product Development*, 283. Courtesy of Fairchild Publications, Inc.

The following is a step-by-step guide to completing a cost sheet:

1. At the top of the form are a group of boxes for information that you have filled in on other forms in the spec pack. Repeat the style number, season, description of the style, fabric, sizes offered, and size scale in the boxes provided. The date that your spec pack will be completed and mailed goes in the upper right-hand corner.

2. A sketch of the front of the garment should be placed in the box provided. It is best to use the same sketch that you have used on your previous forms for this garment.

3. Under the heading Material, enter a short description of each fabric and lining that will be used in your garment. In the next two columns, detail first the number of yards of each component and the appropriate cost per yard. Calculate the cost for each fabric and then a total cost for all materials.

4. The next section is for trims and findings. Trim can be defined as decorative additions to a garment and include lace, ribbon, appliqués, embroidery, and the like. Findings are functional items like buttons, snaps, *rivets*, zippers, etc. Enter each component of your garment separately, the number of pieces of each that will be required, the cost for one piece, and an extension to get the total cost of each, and then a total cost for all trim.

Figure 08.07 is a chart that shows the most common sizes and types of buttons. Buttons are measured in lignes; one ligne is equivalent to $1/40$ of an inch.

5. The Labor section is where you will enter the cost of cutting, sewing, and finishing one garment, plus the cost of all finishes that will be added to the garment after it is sewn, and a total of all labor costs.

6. Shipping costs from your country of origin are to be listed next. We will use a very rough estimate for this cost as the calculation of exact costs is dependent upon a number of factors that vary widely from apparel company to apparel company. Enter a rough estimate here.

Calculating Shipping Costs

Chief among the factors that influence shipping costs are: (a) the weight of the garments to be shipped, (b) the number of units to be shipped, which affects whether the importer will be able to fill an entire shipping container (thus reducing the cost) or will need to share the container's space with another importer, and (c) the shipping time needed in order to be able to deliver the garments to market in a timely manner. The shorter the time frame that can be allotted to getting the goods to the United States, the more expensive will be the shipping costs.

As an example, a direct boat from China following a normal (not expedited) shipping route for medium-weight garments would cost about $8.00 per dozen garments, based on a full container load. From Turkey, that type of shipment would cost about $6.00 per dozen. From Mexico, it would be less expensive because of the shorter distance that the shipment would travel.

Back to the Simulation

7. The next entry is for the charges that will be imposed by the U.S. **Customs** Department for the privilege of importing your garments from the country of origin into the United States. This charge is called duty and the amount of duty that will be applied to your garments is set by the Harmonized Tariff System (HTS), which is controlled by the U.S. International Trade Commission. The reference manual with the information about the duty rates for every item that could conceivably be imported into the United States is the size of an unabridged dictionary. Information about the duty on a particular item can be obtained by logging on to www.dataweb.usitc.gov/scripts/tariff2004.asp. The HTS assigns a category and a number to each item and a percentage duty charge to be levied on the cost of labor and materials for each item that is imported. The current HTS information on blue jeans is as follows:

CATEGORY	CATEGORY #	HARMONIZED #	DUTY RATE
Women	348	6204624010	16.6%
Girls	348	6204624040	16.6%
Men	347	6203424010	16.6%
Boys	347	6203424035	16.6%

8. Overhead is the combination of all other expenses incurred in the manufacturing of each garment. These may vary from company to company; in our example, we have determined that a total of 18 percent of labor plus materials (fabric plus trim and findings) will be assigned. That figure is composed of 7.9 percent for style development costs, 9 percent for administration, and 1.1 percent for financing interest charges.

9. Next we total all manufacturing costs: total material + total trim + total labor + shipping + duty + overhead.

10. To the total manufacturing cost, we must add markup, also called gross margin. Markup goals and requirements differ from company to company. Department stores in today's environment seek to average their markups at approximately 55 percent to 60 percent. Management usually challenges the buyer/product developer to use private-label programs to increase their markups, for it is with these direct-buy programs that the buyer can eliminate the domestic wholesaler and thus realize a greater markup. For our example in Figure 08.05, we have used a markup of 60.6 percent. This markup will cover the following store expenses: 10 percent for markdowns, 2.5 percent for shortages, 40 percent to cover store expenses, 2.5 percent for taxes, and 5.6 percent for net profit.

In order to calculate the retail price, when you know the markup percent goal, you would first find the reciprocal of the markup. In all cases the formula is: Retail (or selling price) represents 100 percent, and if you subtract the markup percent from 100 percent, you will be left with the reciprocal of the markup. In the case of our example in Figure 08.05:

$$
\begin{array}{rl}
& 100\% \\
- & 60\% \text{ (our markup percent goal)} \\
\hline
= & 40\% \text{ reciprocal of markup}
\end{array}
$$

Next we divide the total manufacturing cost by the reciprocal of the markup and that will give us the retail price.

$$
\frac{\$9.84}{.40} = \$24.60 \text{ retail price}
$$

Retail prices are almost always rounded off to the nearest even dollar amount (except for some discount stores that round off to the nearest .99 ending). So, for this example, we will round off our retail price to $25.00 and then recalculate the markup in this manner:

$$
\begin{array}{rl}
& \$25.00 \text{ (retail price rounded off)} \\
- & 9.84 \text{ (total manufacturing cost)} \\
\hline
= & \$15.16 \text{ (markup dollars)}
\end{array}
$$

Snowman multicolor embroidery
Approx. $0.50 each piece
4361 stitches

One-color flower/bow embroidery
Approximately $0.40 each piece
3441 stitches

Stars screen print design with glitter
Cost: about $0.40

FIGURE 08.08

Embroideries and screen print examples

SOURCE: Courtesy of Milco Industries, New York, NY

Then we divide the markup dollars by the retail dollars to get the actual markup percent:

$$\frac{\$15.16}{\$25.00} = 60.6\% \text{ actual markup percent}$$

You may decide that you want to embellish your jeans by adding embroidery or a screen-print design. Determining the cost prices for these elements can be rather complicated and would vary from country to country and resource to resource. As a buyer/product developer working for a store like Perry's, you would have access to suppliers and agents who would provide you with comparative prices for the embellishments you select. For the purpose of the simulation, you can come to a rough estimate for these extras.

Prices for embroidery sewn directly onto a part of a garment or cut pattern piece is based on the number of stitches in a particular design. Prices are quoted as the charge per 1,000 stitches. In China or Turkey, prices for a simple embroidery run about $0.10 to $0.15 per 1,000 stitches. One-color embroideries cost the least; the more colors, the more expensive the embroidery. You can make a rough estimate of the number of stitches in your embroidery by comparing it to a quarter. A simple embroidered design the size of a quarter would contain approximately 2,500 to 3,000 stitches, depending upon the space between the stitches.

Figure 08.08 contains some sample embroideries with their approximate costs. The stars design in this figure is a screen print with glitter.

FINALIZING THE SPEC PACK—WHERE DOES IT GO NEXT?

Now that your spec pack forms are ready, it is time to put them together with the first patterns that have been completed by the production staff at Perry's. First patterns are flat patterns for the sample size only. They are usually created from *slopers* or blocks, which are basic patterns that the company has established as good fit models for their target customers. The first patterns will be used by the contractor to make the prototype sample.

The spec pack forms that the buyer has generated will be distributed to everyone in the Perry's organization who will be responsible for purchasing components, scheduling production, creating patterns, monitoring quality, and ensuring timely shipments. The spec pack minus the cost sheet plus the first patterns will be sent to the overseas contractor. With this information in hand, the contractor can make the prototype (first) samples for construction and fit approval, schedule production, order samples of the fabric and lab dips for color approval, and secure print approval strike-offs of any printed fabrics in the program. The cost sheet would not be sent to the contractor because the information on that form is for the confidential use of Perry's associates.

After the prototype samples are made and returned to the buyer, fit sessions will take place. At that time, garments will be measured for adherence to the size specifications issued. The buyer and pattern-makers will look at the garments on dress forms and (in most cases) on live fit models. The models can provide important insight into the fit, comfort, and feel of each item. During these sessions, the buyer and the pattern-making team will make any necessary adjustments to the original size specifications and note these on the original detail and size specification sheet in the columns marked Revised. When the prototype garments have been revised to everyone's approval, the pattern-making team will begin the process of grading the first pattern up for the larger sizes and down for the smaller sizes in order to finalize size specifications for each of the sizes that will be offered for each style. When these are complete, they will make patterns for each size and then create markers for each style. It is at this stage that the pattern-makers will closely evaluate each style in the collection to see if there are ways to minimize the costs for each component on the preliminary cost sheet. Since fabric (materials) usually account for about 30 percent to 40 percent of the total manufacturing cost of a garment, it is critical that the fabric be utilized in the most efficient manner.

Markers are paper patterns that are usually created by a computerized system that will lay out the pattern pieces in the best way in order to maximize the yield of each yard of piece goods. When the markers are completed to include all pattern pieces for all sizes in the assortment, they will be forwarded to the contractor, who will lay them on the fabric and cut the pieces to be used to make the jeans in your order.

When the overseas contractor sends the prototype samples to the buyer, he or she will also quote a final labor cost (cut, make, and trim cost). After the production department at Perry's has completed all negotiations for the purchase of materials, trim, and findings, and has finalized shipping costs, a final cost sheet can be prepared. The buyer will then need to determine final retail price points for the line of jeans.

CHAPTER 9

WHAT HAPPENS NEXT?

Preproduction and Production Process and Problems

IN THIS CHAPTER, YOU WILL LEARN:

* The production process in a typical contractor's facility
* Some problems that may arise with offshore sourcing
* The extent of the buyer/product developer's involvement in this phase of product completion
* The importance of quality control standards
* How to establish and monitor good *quality assurance*

In the last chapter, we ended our discussion with the importance of careful planning and control in pattern making and marker making in order to minimize fabric waste. Maximizing fabric consumption can be one of the most important steps to improving the gross margin on each item in the buyer's collection.

To that end, there are continual improvements made to computerized marker making that use every possible inch of fabric to best advantage. Today, computers make the patterns and then make the markers. The pattern-maker can store various body shapes from previously used patterns, update them for new styles, define the grading standards, and then run a program overnight that will find the most efficient layout for the markers.

The making of the marker is the last step that Perry's will perform in the production of the garments. Some retailers will have personnel on staff to perform this function; others will outsource it to an independent agency. The markers will then be shipped (or transferred electronically) to the contractor in the selected production country.

When the markers arrive in the contractor's factory, they will be sent to the cutting room, where the fabric that has arrived from the mill is stored. The first step in the construction process is called *spreading* and involves laying the fabric out on the cutting table and positioning the marker over it in order that it may be cut correctly.

Ideally, prior to the arrival of the markers, the fabric rolls would have been checked for defects on an inspection machine. This is a simple, often automatic machine that unrolls the fabric so that inspectors can check for soils, undesirable fabric *slubs*, unacceptable shading of color, uneven or unclear printing, runs, and holes. Usually, the machine is equipped with a light behind the fabric so that these defects are easier to spot. The inspection will most likely begin with a thorough check of 10 percent of the rolls received. Standards will have been set for the number and type of defects allowed. If more than the acceptable level of problems is found, then one of two things will happen: Either the fabric will be returned to the mill for correction or replacement, or the inspection process will be elevated to the level of 100 percent, to determine which rolls can be used and which ones must be eliminated. The decision about which of these steps to take will often depend upon how much time it would take for the mill to replace the entire shipment of fabric.

One of the problems with using offshore contractors is that the Perry's product development team cannot be on hand in the event of a problem with a fabric shipment. Sometimes there is a fine line between whether an entire lot of fabric should be rejected or accepted, and adherence to the ship date can be compromised. It is vitally important that the Perry's buyer and PD team have a strong working relationship with the contractor and that the contractor is fully aware of acceptable quality standards for all phases of construction so that he or she and the team will feel comfortable making critical judgments of pass or fail on fabric lots.

Spreading can be accomplished manually by two workers: one on either side of the table who unroll the bolts of fabric, one *ply* at a time, to the length of the table. As they spread, they will smooth the fabric and also perform a quick eye scan for defects that might have been missed in the fabric inspection. If they find them, they will cut out that portion of the roll of fabric and continue with the spreading operation. Each time they reach the end of the table, they will cut the fabric, then continue rolling until they achieve the desired number of ply (layers) for the fabric and pattern to be cut. Many contract factories around the world still operate a manual spreading system, particularly in parts of the world where labor is inexpensive and plentiful. The more modernized factories have changed over to an automated system. Workers are still required (either one or two) to move the spreader back and forth across the fabric. As the automatic spreader reaches the end of the table, a fabric catcher (usually a metal bar) will grab the fabric, hook it, and hold it down so that the automatic spreader can begin its journey to the other end of the cutting table. Advantages to the automatic spreading system are that fabric tension is correct for the fabric, the edges are more even, and the spreading process can be done more quickly.

Newer computerized spreading machines can even be programmed to lay out the desired ply length that is needed for the marker, roll out the fabric with the exact tension required, and hold down the fabric with a vacuum system so that a preprogrammed cutting machine can cut the pieces. In China and parts of the world where labor is plentiful and inexpensive, these expensive computerized systems would probably not be used.

After the spreading has been done (the number of layers that can be spread at one time depends upon the thickness of the fabric, how slippery it is, and what type of knife is to be used), then the cutting begins. First the paper marker will be laid on top of the stack of fabric. The cutter will then use either a hand-guided electric knife, an electric rotary cutter, or a computerized laser cutter to cut along the pattern lines through the layers of fabric. This is a very important step in production; if it is not done accurately, then the garments will not fit or hang correctly.

After the pattern pieces are cut, they will be carefully tied together (bundled) and a production ticket will be included along with findings, trim, plus brand and care labels that will need to be attached to the garments. This step is also important to the quality assurance program, as mishandling of pieces to be bundled together can result in garments that are made with mixed shades of color.

The bundles are then passed along to the sewing operators for completion. There are several methods of setting up sewing operators to handle the construction process. In many places in the world, the line system is still used. In this method, the bundles are passed down the line in an orderly manner, allowing one sewer to complete one sewing operation before the bundle is then passed to the next operator, who will perform the next required operation in putting together the garment, and so on down the line until the garments are complete.

A newer method of setting up a sewing group is the modular system. Operators are set up in a small group with the machines touching and facing one another in two lines. Instead of using bundles of cut pieces, each garment will have all components together and will be sewn completely in the modular group. Each sewer will perform multiple operations on the one garment before she passes it on to the next operator in her module; thus the operators monitor one another and are very dependent upon one another for the speed in which they are able to produce their garments. The enhanced discipline of the unit makes it much easier to spot errors and to fix them while they are still in the sewing process. Fewer total workers are needed for this method, even up to 50 percent fewer sewers. George Kress, president of Character, Inc., a manufacturer of ladies' sleepwear that just opened a sewing factory in China after more than 30 years of manufacturing in the Dominican Republic and Honduras, has this to say about modular production units: "They are the Rosetta Stone for our manufacturing process, and perhaps 80 percent of the reason that we are opening our own plant in China." Mr. Kress goes on to say that modular systems, however, work best for garments with fewer than 16 sewing operations, so they are not the ideal for most jeans production.

After the garments are sewn, they will be sent to the finishing unit, where several operations will be performed:

1. The final quality control check will take place and garments that need to be mended or discarded will be identified and corrective action will be taken.

2. The finishers will snip loose threads that have been missed in sewing. This is a necessary step, as most retailers and consumers consider too many loose threads to be a quality infraction.

3. At this stage, hangtags and price tickets may be attached.

4. Garments will be ironed or steamed to ensure that there are no unsightly wrinkles. Because of the fabric and the many sewing operations on jeans, they typically require close attention and extra time in the pressing stage.

5. If the order requires that the garments are to be folded and packed for display and selling purposes, that step will be done according to strict guidelines from the customer concerning exactly how each garment is to be folded, whether pins or some other device should be used to secure the garments, and what type of plastic bag or box must be used to enclose them. Most garments (including jeans) are either put on hangers or not according to order directions, put in plastic bags to cover their length, folded once, and then packed into sturdy cartons of 12 to 48 pieces for shipping.

In the final stage of packing, the garments will be put into large steel containers that are either 20 or 40 feet long. It is probable that jeans would be shipped from a place as far away as China in 40-foot containers because of the cost efficiency. A 40-foot container would hold about 21,000 to 24,000 garments, depending upon the bulk of the styles. A second option for packing is to use a container that holds garments on hangers on bars, to avoid excess wrinkling. This method, called GOH or Garment on Hanger, is expensive and would be very unlikely to be used for jeans.

The most efficient way to ship is in full containers; it costs less and saves time in unpacking and repacking at the final destination. If your order, however, is not large enough to fill a container, then you can arrange to share a container with other importers.

After the containers are packed, they will be put on a ship and sent to one of the ports of entry into the United States, where they will be checked in by U.S. customs inspectors. It is crucial that all U.S. Customs laws be followed and that all paperwork that accompanies the shipment is complete and accurate; otherwise, extensive delays can result.

For additional information about the process of shipping and clearing merchandise into the United States, see the textbook *Perry's Department Store: An Importing Simulation.*

Of course, flying the garments to the United States is an option, but one that will only be used in extreme emergencies, as flying heavy garments from any of your chosen overseas manufacturing locations is expensive and will greatly diminish your gross margin on the program.

After the garments have cleared customs, they will likely be put onto a truck or truck/train combination and sent to the Perry's warehouse for distribution to each of the Perry's stores. Sometimes the garments are prepacked in labeled shipping cartons and sent directly to the stores. This can save time and money but eliminates the extra quality check and the extra measure of control that the warehouse personnel can exert in assuring that the right styles, sizes, and colors go to the right stores.

QUALITY CONTROL AND QUALITY ASSURANCE

Random House Dictionary of the English Language defines **quality control** as "a system for verifying and maintaining a desired level of quality in a product or process by careful planning, use of proper equipment, continued inspection, and corrective action as required." In this section, we will deal with all these aspects of the QC process.

The first and most important thing to remember about quality is that it cannot be added at the end of the production process; it must be built into each product when it is first conceived (Keiser & Garner, *Beyond Design*, p. 325). The standards that are set in

TABLE 09.01

CHECKLIST FOR QUALITY STANDARDS

COMPLETION	STEPS	WHO'S RESPONSIBLE
✔	Involve top management	Buyer
✔	Encourage training and education of all employees	Management
✔	Continuously improve processes	All PD team members
✔	Understand that dedication to quality is a positive contributor to the growth and prosperity of the company	Everyone in the company, plus all suppliers of component parts of the garments and contractors
✔	Measure quality attributes	Buyer and quality assurance team
✔	Analyze the variables that cause quality defects	Contractors, suppliers, quality assurance team, buyer
✔	Improve processes to create and produce quality products	All PD team members, plus contractor and suppliers
✔	Control processes so that the same problems do not reoccur	Management, buyer, PD team members, suppliers, contractors

SOURCE: Adapted from Deming's, Juran's, and Harry's concepts concerning the role of quality. Jeremy A. Rosenau and David L. Wilson (2001). *Apparel Merchandising: The Line Starts Here*, 249.

the beginning must then be strictly adhered to and monitored at each stage of the development and production process—from the first product development team meeting to the arrival on the selling floor at Perry's.

The role of standards can be illustrated as follows:

* Used as the basis for the development of product specifications

* Provide guidelines for everyone on the product development team to follow in the execution of the program

* Form the framework of expectations for all suppliers of component parts: fabric, trim, findings; as well as for the contractor who will make the garments and the inspection team who will monitor them

* Allows the company to build in and execute profitable transactions

* Most important, helps to ensure that Perry's customers will be pleased with the look, feel, and performance of the products

Meeting customer expectations and providing them with consistent quality and fit should be uppermost in the mind of the buyer as she or he begins the process of creating a new garment collection, especially a private-label branded program. Perry's name on the label should clearly indicate to the consumer that she or he can expect to experience the level of fit and excellent quality that is promised from all products that bear the company name.

Focus on quality should not just sit with the buyer, however, but be the concern of everyone in the organization, starting with top management. Table 09.01 is a chart of eight key principles upon which to build a quality program.

Quality control is achieved through a strong program of **quality assurance**, or the establishment of a set of rules and guidelines that clearly define expectations and set limits for allowable defects. Those guidelines should identify which defects are considered major and would cause the garment to either undergo extensive correction or be rejected, and which ones are minor. Minor defects might include things such as hanging threads, soils that can be easily cleaned, or a loose button; in other words, defects that do not alter the acceptance or performance of the item. We must also take into account the consumer's perception of quality. Some things, like an uneven hem, may not affect the functionality of the style, but the customer would definitely consider it unacceptable quality (Stamper, Sharp, Donnell, *Evaluating Apparel Quality*, p. 13).

While we understand that quality can have different meanings to different customers, and that it is somewhat dependent upon the price tag that accompanies the garment (higher retail prices should equate with higher quality), we also know that in today's highly competitive marketplace, customers demand quality at all price points. There are certain minimum quality standards that must be present in all garments in order for a consumer to be willing to purchase them; after that, the further definition of quality expectations depends upon the retailer and the customer who shops there.

The most basic expectations of quality can be identified by the following factors:

* Durability—The customer has a right to expect that the garment will last for a reasonable length of time under normal wear and after repeated cleaning.

* Comfort—No customer will want to own a garment that does not fit and feel good against the skin.

* Care—Price can be a determining factor here, as customers will probably not be willing to dry-clean inexpensive items or items that are to be worn often; most commodity items (including jeans) are expected to come with a machine wash label.

* Appearance retention—The consumer wants to be certain that the garment will keep its original look after it is worn and cleaned. In the case of jeans, there is sometimes an exception when fashion dictates that the more worn and torn the style is, the more desirable. This should be at the discretion of the customer, unless the style is manufactured as worn and torn and marketed accordingly.

Quality standards for a particular item or program should be established when the program is first conceived, and specific and clear guidelines should be written and passed along to everyone involved in the process. Some retailers stipulate that contractors must put up posters in the sewing facility with a list of the retailer's quality standards.

We discussed the various quality checks that take place in the factory during production of the items. In addition to these, the buyer will probably want to arrange for certain tests to take place at various points during the production process:

1. When the first run of fabric is complete, the buyer will probably demand that a 2- to 5-yard piece be sent to him or her for lab testing. One to 2 yards will then be sent to a preapproved testing lab to be sure that it matches specifications of colorfastness, wash/care instructions, *tensile strength*, resistance to effects of sunlight and atmosphere, appearance retention after cleaning, shrinkage, and any other standards that have been set down at the beginning of the process.

2. In previous chapters, we discussed the fact that the buyer receives fit samples for approval before production can begin so that any deviations from standard can be recognized and corrected early in the process. Most likely, the buyer would also request a second set of fit samples from the first production run. Because sewing is not an exact science and each garment will have passed through many hands before it reaches the end of the sewing line, it is important to be certain that specification measurements are correct on production garments, and that the jeans fit. When the patterns and markers were sent to the contractor, the Perry's team would have included with their specification measurements a list of the allowable *tolerances*. These are definitions of accept-

able deviations from specified measurements for each of the points on the size specification sheet. They are listed as portions of inches (⅛ inch up to a maximum of 1 inch deviation allowed, depending upon the critical fit of each point of measurement); and they apply to allowances either under or above the desired standard. If more tolerance is taken in the sewing of a garment than what is allowed, fit can be compromised and the garments can be determined to be unacceptable for the Perry's customer. One of the challenges of overseas contracting is the time that it takes to get approval samples from the plant to the buyer, so it is crucial that the buyer take action as soon as first production garments are received to avoid problems with the entire production run. After the fit sessions are complete, the buyer might also choose to send these garments to a lab for additional testing of shrinkage, durability, and appearance retention after cleaning.

3. If Perry's does not employ certified inspectors in the countries (or regions) where the jeans are being made, then they would most likely enlist the services of a contracted inspection agency to make periodic, perhaps even unannounced, visits to the sewing factory to check work in process. There are several very qualified and reliable agencies that perform these services in countries all around the world.

4. Perhaps in a large, important private-label program such as this jeans collection, the buyer might be asked to accompany the inspection team on a visit to the plant to reinforce Perry's commitment to excellence.

5. Even after the goods arrive in Perry's warehouse in the United States, further spot inspections should take place before the goods are repacked and sent to the branch stores.

Testing methods are set primarily by two organizations: the American Association of Textile Chemists and Colorists, which concentrates on colors, dyes, finishes, and *laundry* methods, and the American Society of Testing and Materials (ASTM), whose major concern is product performance. In addition, ASTM publishes the official guide to care symbols called the *Annual Book of ASTM Standards*, which details the symbols for care and cleaning that are understood universally (Figure 09.01).

These are used on care labels for almost all garments manufactured today. The Federal Trade Commission mandates all label requirements and sets the guidelines for

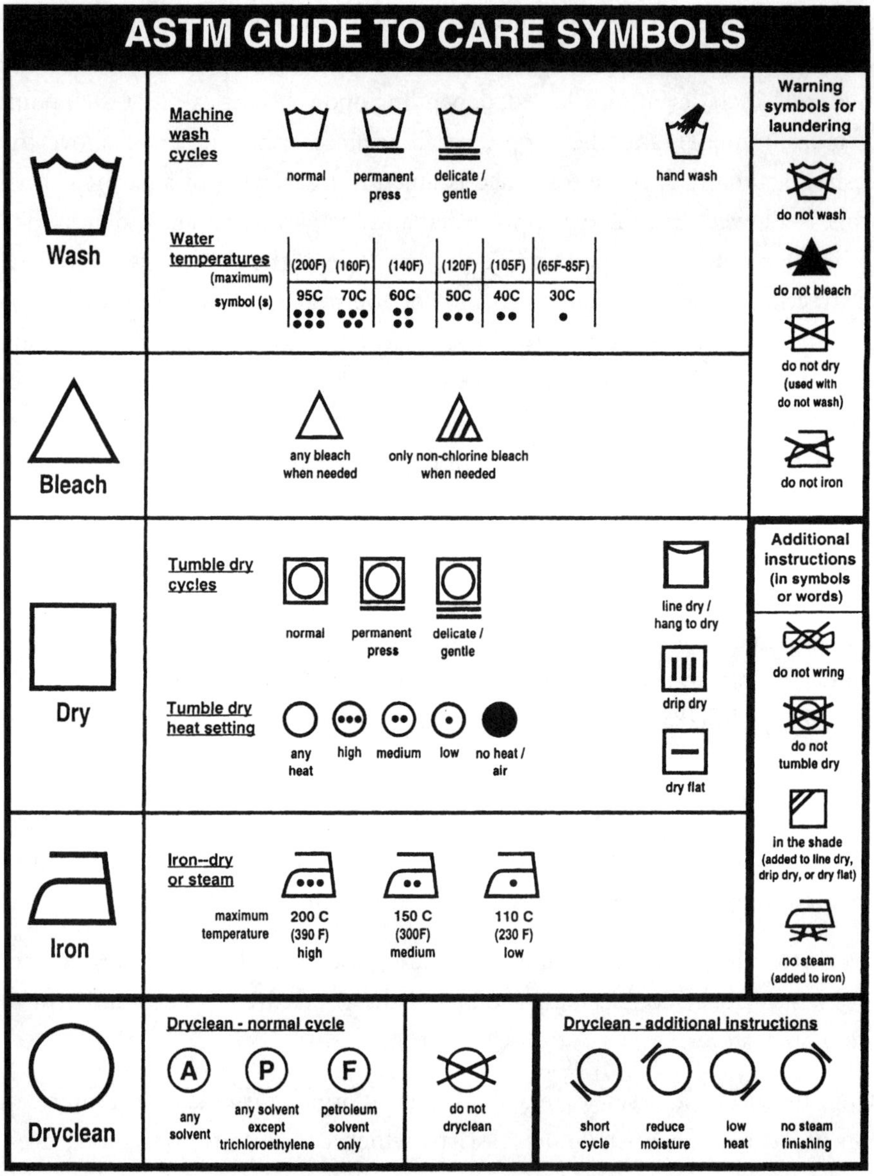

FIGURE 09.01

ASTM guide to care symbols

SOURCE: Copyright 2004 ASTM International, 100 Barr Harbor Drive, West Conshohocken, PA 19428. Extracted, and reprinted from ASTM Standard D5489-01a, with permission of ASTM International. A copy of the complete standard may be purchased from ASTM International, phone: 610-832-9585, fax: 610-832-9555, e-mail: service@astm.org, website: www.astm.org.

fiber content, manufacturer (or retailer) identification number, country of origin, and care instructions. It is vital that the product development team at Perry's have a member who is responsible for knowing all rules and regulations of labeling.

1. Consult the Web site for the Federal Trade Commission and familiarize yourself with 16 CFR part 423, Care Labeling of Textile Wearing Apparel and Certain Piece Goods. This information can be found at www.ftc.gov/os/statutes/textile/carelbl.htm. You will use this information when performing your quality inspection.

SIMULATION:
Go to Table 09.02 in the book and assemble samples.

2. Working in product development teams, assemble several different pairs of jeans that are representative of the jeans that are in your private-label program. As you did in Chapter 8, you may either bring in jeans from the personal wardrobes of PD team members or you may borrow them from a local store.

3. Using Table 09.02, check the jeans for quality defects in the parts detailed there. Find one or more class members (fit models) who are close to the standard size for each of the samples collected and ask them to try on the jeans and comment on fit, feel, and attractiveness.

4. Check the brand labels and the care labels for appearance, comfort, location on the garments, method of attachment, wording, country of origin, and adherence to Federal Trade Commission rules.

5. Compare all garments that you have collected and make a determination of which ones will likely meet customer expectations in all categories. Note areas that should have been corrected before the garments reached the selling floor.

TABLE 09.02

QUALITY CHECK POINTS FOR JEANS

CHECK POINT	CRITERIA
GRAINLINE	This will be easier to see on inside of jean. Check to see that grainline is straight; this will affect look and fit
FABRIC FLAWS	All fabrics have them, but major ones should have been rejected and minor ones should appear on less noticeable parts of jean
SEAMS	Should be flat, even, strong, and have stitch length that is tight enough to hold, but not so tight that seams will pucker
POCKETS	* Openings should be large enough to get hand in & out comfortably * If lining is of a different fabric, it should not show from the outside when sitting or standing * Pocket depth should be adequate, but not so long that the pocket will bunch up * Should be reinforced at corners with bar tacks or backstitching * There should be no puckering or pulling * If there are patch pockets, they should be attached evenly and at the same place on both sides of the jean
WAISTBANDS	* No raw edges; should be cleanly finished inside and out * Belt loops secure, spaced evenly, and identical in size * No evidence of waistband stretching during sewing * Even width around the entire waistband * All closures securely attached and strong enough to hold the parts of the band together
ZIPPERS/PLACKETS	* Zipper should be made of material that is strong enough to hold the fabric together * Length should be suitable for getting into and out of jeans comfortably * All visible stitching should be neat & even * Zipper should be securely attached * Zipper teeth should be covered adequately by flap. Flap should be evenly sewn
HEM	Should be even in depth, flat and smooth with no puckers or pulling, and parallel to the floor unless the styling has an intentional curve
FIT	* Enough ease should have been built into the garment to allow for comfort when moving and sitting (and still be tight enough for attractiveness if the styling dictates) * Overall garment should be free of wrinkles * When viewed on a model or form, all vertical seams should be perpendicular to the floor

SOURCE: Adapted from Anita A. Stamper, Sue Humphries Sharp, and Linda B. Donnell (1991). *Evaluating Apparel Quality*, 2nd Edition, Chapters 2, 5, 8, 9, 10, and 12.

CHAPTER 10

SELLING THE LINE

Marketing and Public Relations

IN THIS CHAPTER, YOU WILL LEARN:

* How to integrate your new program into the stores' existing jean departments
* The importance of good publicity and public relations
* How to work with other departments within the company to achieve your marketing goals for the new collection
* The role of visual merchandising in achieving success with your private-label program
* How to further guarantee success through proper education of and securing enthusiasm and cooperation from the sales staff of each store

Marketing is not just selling the final product, as some may think, but is in fact an entire process that you began the moment that you and your team conceived the idea of developing a private-label brand of jeans. Whether you were aware of it or not, you have been working that process through all the steps that you have thus far taken. When the buyer/product developer decides to add a new collection to an existing line, he or she must make a marketing decision of how that new collection will complement existing product selections, providing an avenue for additional sales and profits without just stealing sales from product already established in the department. True, a buyer often will drop a collection that has shown poor performance in order to free up open-to-buy dollars to purchase a new program to replace the underachiever. The goal, however, always is to achieve add-on sales and/or profits (not just replacement dollars) from any new merchandise that is brought into the department. This evaluation of the needs and best interests of the department and the store was really the first decision in the marketing process.

At the same time that you as buyer/product developer made the decision to add the new private-label collection, you also had to keep in mind the identity and reputation of the Perry's private-label brand name that you planned to use for this program. Perry's has spent many years establishing goodwill with their customers, and good public relations with the community, through the careful planning and monitoring of all merchandise deemed to be worthy of all the Perry's private-label names. As with any brand name that is available to the consumer and against which Perry's must compete, your customer will expect consistent fit and good performance from all items that carry the Perry's private-label name (no matter the category of merchandise or the department in which they are found). Because the private-label names are so important to the store, you would have secured permission from management before using the name, and they would have been involved in the monitoring of your program from beginning to end. Focus group data has shown that customers who have a long-standing, positive experience with a store brand may come to think of that brand as a national brand and equate it to other successful national brands with which they are familiar.

Long before the actual arrival of goods into the stores, the buyer would have worked with other departments at Perry's headquarters to ensure that the marketing and selling of the new collection fit the established profile for that store brand name image. Some of those departments might be:

* Public Relations—to find ways to get the word to the customer at low cost and high credibility. You will want to be sure that press kits and press releases are created to announce your new collection. The buyer/product developer will be asked for input into the creation of these vehicles. The public relations department will then work through their community contacts to attempt to get newspaper articles, radio announcements, and even local TV coverage of the arrival of an exciting new Perry's private-label program.

* Advertising—to decide upon the best course of action and the best allocation of company resources (people, time, money) to use paid methods for getting out the proper message about the new collection.

* Art Department—Before you finalized your specification sheets, you would have worked with the art department on the design of all hangtags and labels to be certain that they are compatible with those that are on other products that carry the Perry's private label that your garments will represent. You will also work with the art department in conjunction with the advertising department to plan and approve any information that is dispensed to the public about your collection.

* Visual Merchandising—to ensure that the layout and look of each branch store's jeans department will be carefully reworked to accommodate the new collection. Decisions must be made about where in the department the new collection should be housed, where existing collections will need to be relocated within the department to make room for the new one, and how the look and shopability of the total department layout can be maximized. The buyer will want to be an important part of this decision-making process.

* Management—to keep them informed and in agreement with all marketing plans for the new private-label collection. A good buyer always wants management on his or her side, and to keep them excited and informed about new offerings.

It is important to recognize that all departments need to work together and depend upon one another in order to achieve the most important goal: to satisfy the needs and expectations of the customer (Swanson and Everett, p. 10).

Although others in the Perry's organization will certainly have influence and involvement in the planning and execution of any new private-label collection, the performance of the product on the sales floor will ultimately be the responsibility and demand the accountability of the buyer/product developer. To that end, the buyer must carefully plan all aspects of the collection's introduction into the department and the company. In Chapter 2, you researched and defined your target customer. Keeping that customer in mind, you should review your plans to make certain that you have satisfied the four P's of marketing that will define the customer's reaction to your offering.

1. Product—The customer will not respond to a product that does not meet his or her expectations or offer a better substitute for other similar products in the marketplace. You have already set the groundwork for this expectation in the careful planning and execution of every step of the product development process. You must continue to monitor the process until all product reaches the sales floor.

2. Place—It is important that the customer enjoys the shopping experience in your stores. The place (Perry's) has been established, but you can control the experience through: (a) working with visual merchandising to create an inviting shopping environment, and (b) interacting with salespeople in all branch stores to make certain that they will provide the kind of service that the customer expects.

3. Price—In your preliminary research on the store, the target customer, the relationship of this new collection to all other jeans in your department, and the offerings of key competitors, you made some decisions about the initial retail price that each item in your collection would carry. You made sure when you worked on cost sheets that these retail prices would provide you with sufficient initial markup to meet company and departmental goals. (Initial markup is the difference between the first selling price and total cost of all materials, labor, and overhead, before any promotional activities such as planned sales and clearance occur to erode the end-of-season *maintained markup*.) It is primarily the role of the buyer to decide how often the price of each item will be reduced and in what format. The buyer must carefully plan how many times during the season and year that the collection will go on sale in order to stimulate sales, knowing that these promotional events will also erode the final gross margin results of the program and his or her department. Remember, however, that customers are most concerned about VALUE. Price is a function of this, but not the whole story. In fact, Price + Quality = Value. The most important feeling that a customer can have after purchasing your product is that she or he received the most value for the most reasonable price.

4. Promotion—To determine how you will inform and excite the customer about your new collection, you will (as previously stated) work with management and the advertising and public relations personnel. To some extent, your opportunities for promoting your product are determined by total company planned promotional events, and certainly by company budgets for these activities. If the company has planned an exciting promotional vehicle (advertisement or special event) that you feel will best showcase your new product, you will want to appeal to the proper department heads to be certain that your new line is included. However, the vehicles for promoting your new collection involve not only advertising and publicity but also how you display your merchandise within your own department and what visual aids and signs you use to capture and inform the customer. These too must be carefully planned and executed.

THE RELATIONSHIP BETWEEN THE BUYER AND THE BRANCH STORES

One of the most important ways that a buyer can impact the success of a new collection is to inform and excite the salespeople who will work directly with the customer. They will provide the final link in the chain from product creation to product acceptance. Never ignore or underestimate the power of a well-informed and motivated sales force. Conversely, if your sales force does not understand and believe in your new collection, they will not inform and excite the customer about it and sales results will likely suffer.

The buyer can motivate and inform the sales staff in a number of key ways:

1. Assuming that Perry's has some kind of regular sales meetings with key branch store personnel, the buyer can use one of these occasions shortly after the collection has been put into production to inform them that an exciting new private-label jean collection is on the way.

2. After promotional vehicles for the introduction of the product have been determined and created, the buyer can share the excitement of this with the sales staff either through a face-to-face meeting or through distribution of written correspondence. The showing of visuals (advertisements, new in-store signs, or publicity pieces, for example) will enhance the effectiveness of this step.

3. Just before the product is due to land in the stores, the buyer should hold a special meeting for the sales staff in all branch stores. If a meeting is not practical, then an informational packet should be created and distributed to each sales associate. The agenda for such a meeting or packet should be to inform the staff of product benefits, explain how the collection will enhance the overall sales of the jeans department, and outline the importance of the role of sales personnel in exciting the customer about the product. This would also be the occasion to introduce any sales incentives that you have designed to reward them for convincing the customer to try the new product. These incentives could come in the form of cash bonuses, gifts, gift certificates, or product samples. This direct interaction with the buyer/product developer serves the dual purposes of giving the salespeople the tools (information) that they need to do the job and motivating them to perform by helping them to understand their personal impact on the success of the new program.

Using the sketches, fabric swatches, and visual elements that you put together for your initial trend boards, create an informational piece for the sales staff.

* Outline the product benefits of each item in your collection.

* Give them information about price, garment care, style, fashionable features, comfort, and any other details that would help them to convince customers to try the items.

* You may also include highlights about the target customer: who will most likely buy the jeans and why.

* Use your own selling skills to excite and motivate them to sell the product.

CHAPTER 11

Career Opportunities in Product Development

IN THIS CHAPTER, YOU WILL LEARN:

* The different types of product development careers and career paths
* The roles, skills, and responsibilities of product development positions in both a retail and a wholesale setting
* Where product development positions reside within an organization and whether they are either design or merchandising based

This chapter details the numerous jobs that can be found in the product development field. The information is synthesized from many different sources to represent careers within retail and wholesale organizations, and looks at positions that tend to be both design versus merchandising based. Every organization defines the responsibilities of product development positions differently, and they also use job titles independently. These job descriptions are generalized but offer a fair representation of the nature of the different careers. This chapter also provides a discussion of training programs and internship opportunities for new graduates.

OVERVIEW

The retail buying positions in today's marketplace are changing so that product development receives greater emphasis. Every organization handles product development differently but many retailers expect buyers to have knowledge of the process and be able to work with designers or manufacturers to produce private–label goods for their department. The following positions, beginning with entry level and moving up through an organization, deal primarily with buying positions from a merchandising perspective.

MERCHANDISING-ORIENTED POSITIONS FOR RETAIL ORGANIZATIONS

Assistant Buyer

The assistant buyer supports the buyer in all aspects of the business, including vendor and store communication, product and customer analysis, delivery of goods, purchase order from inception to completion, and reports detailing sales, sell-through, gross margin, key selling items, reorder items, and slow sellers. The assistant might analyze sales data or customer information to improve consumer-base knowledge or best sellers. Buying assistants may sit on the product development team offering insight based on the many reports and the information that they manage. They also work closely with advertising requests and obtaining samples of both private-label and **branded merchandise**.

QUALIFICATIONS An assistant buyer must be detail oriented and organized. They must be able to multitask and possess excellent analytical skills with the ability to express themselves both orally and with the written word. Computer experience is a must and Word, Excel, and Access software programs are in high demand.

Associate Buyer, Senior Assistant Buyer

The next position before reaching buyer is an associate or senior assistant buyer. This position is usually for a larger organization or for a larger department, and requires managing and buying a specified area. Responsibilities would include pricing and promotional strategy development, a six-month dollar plan, and identification of market and fashion trends for private-label opportunities. They would also work with product development teams or manufacturers to develop private-label merchandise.

Buyer

The buyer is responsible for planning and managing his or her merchandise assortments as well as achieving department financial objectives (sales and gross margin). They are held accountable for sales, markdowns, gross margin, and turnover goals. The buyer understands the customer with regard to lifestyle, attitudes, and values and translates that knowledge into merchandise assortments. They create and maintain relationships with store managers, vendors, product development teams, and allocators while supervising assistant buyers and clerical staff.

QUALIFICATIONS To become a buyer, a minimum of two years of experience is required, depending on the size of the organization. A bachelor degree is strongly recommended, with experience in the following areas: forecasting, merchandise and *strategic planning*, excellent analytical skills, good written and oral communication skills, and the ability to negotiate positive outcomes. A buyer must be very detail-oriented, organized, and have the ability to manage many tasks at once. A working knowledge of finance is very important.

VERTICALLY ORIENTED RETAILER OR MANUFACTURER

Merchandiser

Larger organizations that manage a vertical operation that manufactures private-label merchandise for their own stores have positions such as merchandiser. These jobs provide leadership to store divisions by managing core vendor business, including private brands, delivery of sales, and gross margin results. They require the ability to think strategically.

Key responsibilities of a merchandiser include: monitoring merchandise performance such as private-label programs, sales, margins, merchandise history, and key items; identifying merchandising trends; analyzing customer profiles; and developing seasonal strategies and business objectives that support brand objectives.

QUALIFICATIONS This job requires a bachelor degree in a related field and a minimumof two years of buying experience. This position also requires: Microsoft Office and Excel computer skills; analytical, managerial, negotiating, and strategic planning skills; and excellent communications skills.

Product Manager, Merchandise Manager, Merchandise Product Director

The product manager, merchandise manager, or merchandise product director is responsible for monitoring the performance of merchandise by style and program. This requires the analysis of current and historical sales and market trends to assist in line development meetings, and finalizing style placements on an item and classification basis. The product manager ensures the deadlines are met with regard to each step of the product development process and manages the communication between suppliers, overseas offices, and factories. He or she also develops negotiating strategies to achieve strategic markup goals.

On a more technical basis, the merchandise manager might confirm material selection and shipping, and manage production scheduling and costs. Product fit and maintaining quality standards as well as sample management may be part of this position.

QUALIFICATIONS A bachelor degree in related areas is required, with an extensive knowledge of retail buying and product development. Product managers must have a clear understanding of the target customer, merchandise trends, and financial factors such as gross margin and sell-through. Five to seven years of buying experience or product development as well as two to four years of management experience is preferred.

Senior Merchandiser

This career position leads a product design team in the development of seasonal market and fashion trends for a specific area or brand. The senior merchandiser manages store assortments, promotional strategies, and key concepts, ensuring that each collection meets the consumer demand. They also lead the team in formulating pricing strategies and presenting assortment plans to senior management.

QUALIFICATIONS Senior merchandisers must have a bachelor degree and possess five to seven years of buying or product development experience. They must have a deep knowledge of product trends, strong presentation and communication skills, and an understanding of the offshore production process. They must also have in-depth knowledge of financial considerations such as gross margin, sell-through, and pricing strategies. Senior merchandisers must be able to formulate long-term strategies and short-term adaptive plans to maximize efficiencies.

Vice President of Merchandising

The responsibilities of the vice president focus on the development of long-term strategies and the maximization of earnings. By working closely with cross-functional product development teams, the VP ensures a cohesive presentation of product assortments between all departments and sets price strategies for competitive opportunities. He or she also keeps upper management informed of seasonal investments and ensures that quarterly financial targets are met.

QUALIFICATIONS The VP of merchandising must have a vision and be able to formulate long-term strategies to meet organizational goals. He or she must have a bachelor degree and 10 to 15 years of buying experience, five or more years of management experience, and executive leadership experience. Excellent communication, management, and leadership skills are essential, as well as the ability to motivate and direct a multifunctional team.

DESIGN-ORIENTED POSITIONS

Assistant Designer

An assistant designer would be part of a product development team and be responsible for preparing basic flat sketches and assisting in the development of basic product specifications. He or she would assist in tracking the samples and attend fittings, making revisions as directed by the product manager or designer. He or she would be responsible for the development of presentation boards and tech packs. The assistant designer must have a working knowledge of the product development process.

QUALIFICATIONS Assistant designers must have a degree in fashion design or a related area and have basic knowledge of the following areas: product development, textiles, garment construction, design techniques, and color theory. Skills needed include flat sketches and basic computer knowledge. However, advanced technology in CAD systems or online spec programs is highly recommended.

Associate Designer

As part of the product development team, the associate designer prepares flats and assists with product specification sheets. He or she coordinates sample production and assists in fitting the garment and making appropriate adjustments. The associate designer might assist in the production of tech packs and presentation boards, as well as researching market trends.

QUALIFICATIONS A college degree in fashion design is required, with two plus years' experience. The associate designer must have working knowledge of construction and the product development process. He or she must understand all the concepts including color, design, fit, fabrication, finishes, trim, stitches, etc. Time-management skills are essential as well as computer skills, especially CAD systems.

Designer

A designer holds full responsibility for the entire product development process, including sketching, designing, completion of specification sheets and tech packs, sourcing, and awareness of global fashion and market trends. He or she takes the lead in the conceptualization of the product line and provides leadership to meet organizational timelines and business goals.

QUALIFICATIONS A designer for a product development organization must have extensive design experience and in-depth knowledge of the product development process. He or she must be able to design an entire line based on conceptual presentations and work with new CAD technology. With excellent management skills, he or she must lead the product development process from beginning to end, maintaining the integrity of the merchandising plan as it relates to sales and margin.

Color Analyst

The major responsibilities for a color analyst are creating seasonal color palettes for an entire organization or product line and acting as a liaison between design, merchandising, and textile selection. He or she would also be responsible for maintaining a color library and creating a color swatch or storybook for all buyers, product developers, and/or designers.

QUALIFICATIONS A color analyst is required to have five plus years' experience in textile/color analysis and have a bachelor degree in color theory or a related area. He or she must have in-depth knowledge of color systems such as Greytag or Sectro and possess excellent written and verbal communication skills.

Senior Director of Product Design or Development

A senior director of product design/development manages the entire staff of designers and merchandisers that brings products to market. He or she ensures that the process, including market research, creative direction, specing, fit, fabrication, trim, and sampling, is accurate and timely. The senior director provides vision and continually looks for opportunities to improve and grow the business. He or she is responsible to a vice president of design or product development.

QUALIFICATIONS An extensive knowledge of fashion design combined with management experience is essential for this position. The director position requires excellent management, communication and negotiation skills, with a degree in fashion design or a related area. He or she must be able to motivate and lead a diverse group of professionals to meet organizational goals. Minimum experience in design or product development of ten years is usually required.

Glossary

acid wash A washing treatment of denim using pumice stones soaked in various chemicals to create a mottled and uneven appearance.

antiquing A treatment that incorporates stonewashing, sandblasting, and grinding to create a worn appearance.

bar tacks Tightly placed stitches used to reinforce stress points on jeans.

blocks A company's set of basic patterns for each of the garment types that it produces.

branded merchandise Products created under a "label" that is owned exclusively by an organization. Merchandise is produced and sold to retailers for resale. Designer labels such as Ralph Lauren or Donna Karan are branded merchandise.

broken twill A manufacturing process that alternates the twill line from right to left. This reduces the twist effect due to fabric torque that is common in jeans.

bull denim A cotton twill dyed to look like denim.

bundling During production, the process of tying cut pieces of a style together in preparation for sewing. This is usually done in multiples: For example, all the parts for 6 or 12 garments may be bundled together.

calendering A finishing process for fabric that improves the hand (feel), creating a softer, smoother fabric that accepts more saturated colors.

care label A permanent label, either printed or woven, that must be affixed to the inside of each garment made and must remain legible for the life of the garment. The information to be found on this label concerns the care and cleaning of the garment plus any applicable warnings.

chambray A lighter-weight, plain-weave fabric with an indigo warp often used for shirting.

cowboy cut A style of jeans that includes a tapered leg to fit over boots and back pockets placed high on the buttocks. Originally used by miners in California.

cost sheet The form used by an individual company to detail each of the costs that go into a particular style: fabric, findings, trim, manufacturing costs, transportation, duty, overhead, and profit.

customs A government agency that sets and monitors import regulations, and collects duty (tax) on imported items.

cut, make, and trim (CMT) A method of contract sewing that includes the cost to cut, sew, and finish a garment, including the cost of trim. Design, patterns, and fabrics are provided by the contracting company.

dungaree A term that is used synonymously with denim to describe pants or overalls made from a piece of dyed or solid-colored twill.

duty The tax on imports levied by the government.

enzyme washing A process used to create stonewashed jeans. Enzymes destroy part of the denim, leaving the white core of the denim yarn. This process is often combined with pumice-stone washing.

fabric consumption The number of yards of fabric that it takes to manufacture a particular style.

fabric weight The ounces per square yard of fabric. Denim is usually between 4 and 15 ounces per yard.

findings Additions to a garment that are not fabric and that serve a function to the wearability of the garment. Examples are buttons, grippers, zippers, and elastics.

finishing The final process in the manufacturing of a garment. This includes clipping hanging threads, pressing, folding, and bagging if needed, or placing on a hanger. Quality inspection is usually a part of this process.

flats Mechanical drawings or sketches of garments without bodies. They illustrate details to ensure accuracy in construction.

full package (FP) A form of sourcing or contracting in which the contractor provides fabric, trim, supplies, and labor.

garment dye A dyeing process that creates intense color due to saturation of the fabric. The process is completed in the garment form rather than on the bolt.

grade The difference in measurements between sizes.

grade rules The formula for making patterns for every size, based on a sample size pattern.

grading The process of creating patterns for all of the sizes of a style, based on a sample size pattern and predetermined variances between measurements of each size.

grommets Rings or eyelets, usually made of metal, that originally were designed as functional additions to denim jeans to hold pockets more securely to the garments. While still serving a function, grommets today can also be used as decorative features, sometimes communicating a brand name.

gross margin Net sales minus the total cost of goods sold. Can be expressed in dollars, or as a percentage of total sales.

hand The feel of a fabric to the touch.

hand sanding A process that creates a wear pattern that normally occurs naturally through long-term use.

hipster jeans Jeans that rest 10 centimeters below the waist.

indigo A substance found in plant material that is used to dye fabric. It creates bright hues of blue but is synthesized from chemicals today.

inseam The inside vertical seam of a pant leg.

jeans A style of pants that includes five pockets and is usually made of denim or a cotton-twill weave. They were originally used as work clothing because of their durability. Today, jeans are made from a wide range of fabrication.

lab dip The first approval sample of a color mix. Fabric of the type to be used in the finished garment will be "dipped" into the dye mixture and sent to the buyer/product developer for approval or change.

labor The part of a cost sheet that identifies the total price of the sewing operations that go into the manufacturing of the garment.

laundry A manufacturing facility that treats unwashed jeans to create special appearances such as stonewashing, sandblasting, acid washing, or garment dyeing.

left-hand twill A weave of denim that creates a softer feel by producing the twill line to rise to the left.

maintained markup Markup after all reductions are taken. Reductions include markdowns, stock shortages, and employee and customer discounts.

marker A paper pattern that has been created, either manually or by machine, from the pattern pieces for each style. This paper pattern is then laid down on the stacked fabric to provide a template for cutting the pieces for the garment.

marketing All activities involved in the transfer of goods from seller to consumer; primarily advertising and selling.

markup The difference between the cost of a style and its selling price. This figure is always expressed as a percentage.

mercerization A process used on fabrics or yarns to encourage them to take dye more easily and to have a more lustrous appearance. Mercerized denim lays flat and has a smooth hand.

open-end spinning A less expensive way to spin yarn for denim. The yarns produced are more coarse and not as strong as ring-spun yarns.

outseam The exterior, vertical seam on the outside leg of a pant.

overhead Also known as SGA (Selling, General, and Administration) expenses. These are all expenses over and above the cost of materials, labor, transportation, and duty that are incurred in order to produce a garment.

ply A layer of fabric.

preshrunk A process that pretreats the fabric or garment so that it will shrink less than 3 percent in the laundering process.

print repeats The horizontal and vertical points at which a continuous print, when applied to cloth, will start to repeat itself.

private label A collection of products created by a particular company under its owned label. The purpose of such a collection is for company exclusivity, cost control, and quality regulation.

profit The difference between the total of all costs incurred in the manufacturing of a garment and the selling price.

profit margin The percentage of total sales that is profit.

prototype The first sample of a new style. It is made to give the buyer/product developer the opportunity to see how the style will look and fit when made up into the same or similar fabric.

pumice stones Volcanic stones used in the stonewashing process to create a certain color or texture on denim.

quality Grade of excellence. Each product development company sets its own standards for quality.

quality assurance The process of monitoring and controlling the quality standards that are set for the product; the establishment of a set of rules and guidelines that clearly define expectations and set limits for allowable defects.

quality control A system for verifying and maintaining a desired level of quality in a product or process by careful planning, use of proper equipment, continued inspection, and corrective action.

quota Government-regulated limits on the number of units, kilograms, or square meters, by category, that can be imported each year.

rigid denim Unwashed denim.

ring dyeing The process of dyeing that does not allow for full penetration of color to the inner core of the denim. This allows the white core to appear after finishing or through the natural stress of continuous wear.

ring spinning A process used to spin fine-count yarns, resulting in a more uneven but stronger and smoother yarn than that produced by open-end spinning.

rivet The round metal accessory used to reinforce pockets and stress points or for ornamentation on jeans.

S twist The direction that fibers are twisted within a yarn, creating a "S" pattern when viewed from the side.

sandblasting A process that sprays sand or chemicals to create a worn look on denim.

sand wash A washing process that creates a faded appearance and soft feel.

slim-leg fit A snug-fit jean that hugs from the thigh to the knee.

slopers A set of patterns that account for each basic garment type that a particular company produces.

slub A soft nub in fabric that is either an imperfection or intended to give a denim texture. If intentional, it is regular in size and repetition.

spandex A man-made fiber used to add stretch and recovery to denim and other fibers.

specification package A collection of documents that detail all the expectations for the manufacturing of a garment, including (but not limited to) size specifications, materials, findings and trim, sewing instructions, quality assurance, patterns, and markers.

spreading The step in the production process that involves the preparation for the cutting of the fabric. The fabric is laid out on a cutting table in multiple layers and then the paper marker is positioned on top of the layers so that the cutting process may begin.

strategic planning The first stage of product development, in which decisions are made concerning the allocation of company resources.

stonewash A finishing technique used to produce fabrics with a certain color or texture. Stones are used as an abrasive in the tumbling process.

strike-off The first printing (usually done with a hand-screen printing process) of a new pattern on cloth. The purpose is to give the buyer/product developer a first view to either approve or change.

style number A designator that identifies a particular style. It can be numbers, letters, or some combination of the two.

tensile strength Resistance of a material to longitudinal stress. Measured by the amount of stress needed to rupture or tear the fabric.

tolerances Definitions of acceptable deviations from specified measurements for each of the points on the size specifications standards.

topstitching Heavier yarns or thread used on the outside of a garment for the purposes of decoration, a flatter appearance, and a sturdier seam.

trim Parts of a garment that are typically decorative and not functional. Examples are embroidery and lace.

twill The weave of the S twill or left-hand twill that forms a diagonal line.

warp The lengthwise yarns that are woven over and under the weft, or horizontal yarns. Warp yarns tend to be stronger and twisted because they are subjected to more stress in the manufacturing process.

weave The combination of weft and warp weaves to create different types of designs.

weft The horizontal, crosswise yarns that act as filling to the warp.

yarn dyed A method of dyeing cloth whereby the individual yarns are subjected to a dye bath of the appropriate color, and then the dyed yarns are woven or knit into fabric. This method is especially preferred for stripes and plaids and for solid colors where strong hues or depth of hue is desired.

Z twist The direction of the fibers when twisted creates a "Z" pattern.

Bibliography

Abend, Jules. "The modern definition of 'quality,' (Quality Assurance & Meeting Retail Requirements)," *Bobbin*, June 2002, 34–35.

"At a Premium: The evolution of niche jean trend impacts denim market." *Lifestyle Monitor*, Cotton Incorporated, July 31, 2003.

Bell, Judith, and Kate Ternus. *Silent Selling*. 3rd ed. New York: Fairchild, 2005.

Bryant, Michelle Wesen, and Diane DeMers. *The Spec Manual*. 2nd ed. New York: Fairchild, 2005.

Cone Denim. "Denim 101, What makes denim . . . denim?" www.cone.com/us/denim/101.html (accessed August 16, 2004).

"Denim Chronicle: No Uncertain Terms." *Women's Wear Daily*, June 24, 2004, 22–23.

Cone Denim. "Denim glossary." www.cone.com/us/denim/denimglossary.html (accessed August 14, 2004).

Cone Denim. www.cone.com/us/denim/denimglossary.html

"Denim in Depth: Taking Mexico's Measure." *Women's Wear Daily*, May 27, 2004, 14.

"Denim Jeans Command Loyalty." *Textile Consumer*, Volume 33, Summer 2004, Cotton Incorporated, 1–4.

"Denim Jeans: This Fashion Favorite Won't Fade Away." *Lifestyle Monitor*, Cotton Incorporated, February 2004, 1–3.

"Denim: The Beat Goes On." *Bobbin*, April 2001, 54.

Guthrie, Karen M., and Cynthia W. Pierce. *Perry's Department Store: A Buying Simulation for Juniors, Men's Wear, Children's Wear, and Home Fashion/Giftware*. 2nd ed. New York: Fairchild, 2003.

"Injeanuity: New denim designs command top dollar." *Lifestyle Monitor*, Cotton Incorporated, June 3, 2004.

Jeans Manufacturers. www.jeans.information.in.th/jeans.html

"Jean Therapy—Women continually turn to denim as a fashion favorite." *Lifestyle Monitor*, Cotton Incorporated, March 11, 2004.

Johnson, Maurice J., and Evelyn C. Moore. *Apparel Product Development*. New Jersey: Prentice-Hall, 2001.

Just-style.com. "Calculating accurate fabric costs." www.just-style.com (accessed October 23, 2003).

Just-style.com. "Educating Students for a Global Industry." www.just-style.com, May 3, 2004.

Just-style.com. "Mastering the Process of Merchandising." www.just-style.com, accessed by July 28, 2003.

Just-style.com. "Private Label: the State of the Market." www.just-style.com, accessed by February 2003.

Just-style.com. "The top 8 shopping trends." www.just-style.com/features, (accessed June 28, 2004).

Keiser, Sandra J., and Myrna B. Garner. *Beyond Design: The Synergy of Apparel Product Development*. New York: Fairchild, 2003.

Lurker, Allison. "No Uncertain Terms." *Women's Wear Daily*, June 24, 2004, 22-23.

"Measuring Brand Premium." *Textile Consumer*, Cotton Incorporated, Volume 1, Winter 2003, 1-4.

"Me, Myself and I: The Return of Individual Style." *Lifestyle Monitor*, Cotton Incorporated, Fall 2004, 8.

Myers-McDevitt, Paula J. *Complete Guide to Size Specification and Technical Design*. New York: Fairchild, 2004.

"New Classics: Jeans designers are updating an old standard." *Lifestyle Monitor*, Cotton Incorporated, March 7, 2002.

Nordstrom. "The Perfect Fit, Our Jeans Guide for Women." www.store.nordstrom.com/category/cat_boutique-medium.asp?, accessed February 2004.

Rosenau, Jeremy A., and David L. Wilson. *Apparel Merchandising: The Line Starts Here*. New York: Fairchild, 2001.

"See You in September: Denim Still Going Strong for Fall." *Lifestyle Monitor*, Cotton Incorporated, Fall 2004, 7.

Stamper, Anita A., Sue Humphries Sharp, and Linda B. Donnell. *Evaluating Apparel Quality*. 2nd ed. New York: Fairchild, 1996.

Stone, Elaine. *The Dynamics of Fashion*. 2nd ed. New York: Fairchild, 2004.

Swanson, Kristen K., and Judith C. Everett. *Promotion in the Merchandising Environment*. New York: Fairchild, 2000.

The Fashiondex. *The Apparel Design and Production Hand Book*. New York: The Fashiondex, Inc., 2001.

Williams, Robin. *The Non-Designer's Design Book*. 2nd ed. California: Pearson, 2004.

Undersecretariat of the Prime Ministry for Foreign Trade. www.dtm.gov.tr/English/doing/igout/textile.htm

United States International Trade Commission. www.dataweb.usitc.gov/scripts/tariff2004.asp

Index